ONE
COMPULSIVE EATER HELPING
ANOTHER

WOMEN, FOOD, EATING & LIFE ISSUES

INCLUDED IN THIS 2012 EDITION—

PHONE MEETING HELP · ONLINE MEETING HELP
SPONSORS · FORUMS · PHONE BUDDIES · ACTION PARTNERS
ONLINE DISCUSSIONS · PODCASTS
ORGANIZATION · FREE LITERATURE

Contents

Phone Meetings

Face-to-Face Meetings

Sponsors Phone Buddies

Email Resource

Literature

Organizations

Women Food Eating & Life Issues -
One Compulsive Eater Helping Another -
Phone Meeting Help- Online Meeting Help - Sponsors-Phone Buddies -
Face-to-Face Meetings - Online Discussions - Podcasts
- Organizations - Free Literature and more

By Anonymous Twelve Step Recovery Members

Cover Design: Cheryl Klinginsmith
(c) 2010 All Rights Reserved

Partnerships for Community
561 Hudson Street, Suite 23
New York, N.Y. 10014

Printed in United States

ISBN-978-1-933639-64-2
ISBN-1-933639-64-4

Library of Congress Cataloguing in Publication Data Pending

Women Food Eating & Life Issues -
One Compulsive Eater Helping Another -
Phone Meeting Help- Online Meeting Help - Sponsors-
Phone Buddies - Face-to-Face Meetings - Online Discussions
- Podcasts - Organizations - Free Literature and more
By Anonymous Twelve Step Recovery Members

ISBN 978-1-933639-64-2
ISBN 1-933639-64-4 1.

INTRODUCTION

Now in one place, learn where to find free **Phone Meeting Help - Online Meeting Help - Sponsors-Phone Buddies - Face-to-Face Meetings - Online Discussions - Podcasts - Free Literature - and more** with one compulsive eater helping another in *Overeaters Anonymous Inc.; Compulsive Overeaters Anonymous - HOW; Food Addicts Anonymous; Anorexics & Bulimics Anonymous; The Recovery Group; Greysheeter's Anonymous; 12 Steps for Compulsive Overeaters; Recovery from Food Addiction; OA Primary Purpose; The Coffee Shop; The Parking Lot; and Cups & Scales.* Each organization described here is independent and not affiliated with any other. You will learn distinguishing features of each type of help and in each circle of people, including if the group has a suggested plan of eating and how to find it. This resource provides information. It serves the function of "press." Geneen Roth suggests connection breaks isolation in *Women Food and God.* People are the instrumentalities. "One compulsive eater helping another" in each of these independent organizations is the heart and soul. With information in this book, you will be able to get started with free phone meetings, sponsor-phone buddy lists, and other resources available.

Connecting from home is possible. There are over 150 free phone meetings a week. People dial in from home, from car or work. They speak their truth. People from the U.S. and other countries come together. They communicate and problem-solve in new ways. Others can be counted on, as food never could be, for answers, comfort, and good solid companionship. People are a great resource - one of the greatest resources. We learn from others like us and others different from us, yet similar.

The help described is non-commercial. People do not charge money. Anonymous individuals who practice Twelve Step Recovery decided to produce this yellow pages. It does not endorse or promote any single organization, method or approach; it is neither endorsed nor sponsored by any organization.

You will find people who share about obsession with body size, weight and shape; eating binges; grazing; preoccupation with reducing diets, starving; restricting; excessive exercise; inducing vomiting after eating; use of diet pills, laxatives or diuretics, use of other diet remedies, including bariatric surgery, lap band surgery, weight-loss surgery; vulnerability to quick weight-loss schemes; magical thinking about weight loss; food fantasies or romancing the food; isolation in food; guilt and remorse about eating behaviors and other behaviors. There is no single remedy espoused for all. People follow their own process.

Individuals speak for themselves...

Individuals participate with their own opinions, their own experience. Some circles of people are founded on spiritual-based 12 Step recovery. They offer three-fold help – physical, emotional and spiritual. They also help with "the phenomenon of craving," "food allergies," and "food addiction." Daily or moment-by-moment contact with another human being can help.

The human element makes people happy...

People share wisdom, experience and friendship. Sponsors, phone buddies and action partners volunteer to help others. A Sponsor is someone who will help you to learn about yourself, your life issues, and your eating, by drawing on their own experience and answers.

The spiritual element makes many happy...

There are no weigh-ins. People are more than their body size or weight – they are whole people and share as whole people.

The social element makes people happy...

People make meaningful friendships and break isolation. Phone meetings, phone number and email lists of people volunteering to help make it possible for outreach and communication. People get to know one another in sharing. Respect is a great beginning to friendship. We "hear" others.

The individual learning process makes people happy...

People begin where they are. They learn individually. They learn what they need to learn from others. They follow their own process. It may not be overnight.

The non-commercial element makes people happy...

The participants do not charge money. It does not cost money to dial into a free phone meeting, especially if you have unlimited free long distance. Online meeting are free. Joining an online discussion group from your computer, listening to a free recording, or attending a face-to-face meeting are also free. There is a lot of free literature you can read or download from your computer. There are no weigh-ins or counting calories. There are no foods to buy with shipping fees.

There is wisdom on the wires. Learning how to do life one day at a time comes with being honest and open with at least one other human being. We are not all weak in the same spots or at the same time.

We do not have to go it alone. We can talk about ourselves as we really exist. Help is offered in free, person-to-person, and group connections. 'One compulsive eater helping another' is the heart and soul.

Do I Need a Computer?

No. It helps. A computer is not necessary. With the information in this book, you will be able to get started with phone meetings. We provide phone numbers and access PINs to get started. At phone meetings you can ask for phone number and email lists.

A computer allows you to go to websites listed in this book to get more detailed information. With a computer, you can join email discussion groups and post and share with email participants. With a computer, you may download free literature and free recordings. With a computer, you may attend online meetings with chat or Internet SKYPE phone and online discussion groups.

Do I Need a Phone?

No. It helps. A phone is not necessary. With information in this book, you will be able to write or email for information on face-to-face meetings, or attend online meetings, online discussion groups, and get free literature and recordings from your computer.

With a phone, landline or wireless, you can dial into free phone meetings. If you have unlimited long distance calling plan, your calls will be free. If you have specified minutes on your calling plan, your calls will be within those minutes.

With a phone, you can dial in to a phone meeting or call your Sponsor, Sponsee, Phone Buddy, Action Partner, or any other person-to-person contact, from home, car or workplace.

Do I Need to Go out of My Home?
Can I Get this Help from Car and Work?

You can dial in to a phone meeting, or call your Sponsor, Sponsee, Phone Buddy, Action Partner, from home, car or workplace. You can go to online meetings or join online discussion groups from your home computer.

What are Online Meetings?

Online meetings are free meetings you can attend by going to website addresses or Internet SKYPE phone listed in this book. They last one hour usually. They are moderated by a moderator. They take place at specific times. There may be a speaker. There is open sharing by people attending the meeting.

With information in this book, you will be able to get started.

What are Phone Meetings?

Phone meetings are free meetings of other compulsive eaters, lasting one hour usually. They are moderated by a moderator. They take place at specific times. Meetings follow a format. There may be a speaker. There is open sharing by people attending the meeting. Many types of phone meetings are described in this book.

With the information in this book, you will be able to get started with phone meetings. We provide phone numbers and access PINs to get started. At phone meetings you can ask for phone number and email lists of volunteers willing to help and receive outreach calls. There are over 150 phone meetings a week. Phone meetings and open discussion are available 24 hours a day.

Meetings start as early as 6:45 a.m. EST. Open discussion is available from 1 a.m. to 6:30 a.m. for night eaters, people who eat in the middle of the night, all night workers who are up, people who are lonely, and people who want help from another compulsive eater. You may adjust times given in this book and on websites for your timezone.

With a phone, landline or wireless, you can dial into free phone meetings. If you have unlimited long distance calling plan, your calls will be free. If you have specified minutes on your calling plan, your calls will be within those minutes.

What are Phone Marathons?

Phone Marathons are all-day phone meetings. They are held on Holidays. Where food is often the center of attention on holidays, Phone Marathons offer an opportunity for people to dial in, before or after dealing with food, family and events. The Phone Marathon meetings offer an opportunity for people to center on something other than food on the Holiday and connect with others who are not centered on food.

With the information in this book, you will be able to dial-in to Phone Marathons. We provide phone numbers and access PINS to dial into Phone Marathons on all Holidays.

We provide email addresses to get a list of Holidays dates when Phone Marathons will be held during the upcoming year.

What are Face-to-Face Meetings?

Face-to-Face meetings are free meetings of other compulsive eaters, lasting one hour usually, and moderated by a moderator. They take place at specific times. They take place at specific face-to-face locations in U.S. and International cities and states. Meetings follow a format. There may be a speaker. There is open sharing by people attending the meeting.

With the information in this book, you will be able to write or email for information on face-to-face meetings, or go to websites given to get information on face-to-face meetings offered by the resource.

At face-to-face meetings, you can ask for a list of phone numbers and emails of people who volunteer to help. You can ask for a Sponsor, Phone Buddy or Action Partner.

Where do I get Names of People to help me – phone numbers & email addresses - contact information?

With the information in this book, you will be able to get started. We provide phone numbers, emails and mailing addresses where you may call, write or email for the names of people who volunteer to help and give and receive outreach calls. The names of people with their phone numbers and emails who volunteer to help will be provided to you.

At phone meetings, online meetings, face-to-face meetings, and online discussion groups, you can ask for a list of names, phone numbers and emails for people who volunteer to help. You can ask for a Sponsor, Phone Buddy or Action Partner. You may call and email individuals and get to know them. Talk to them.

What is an Online Discussion Group?

Online discussion groups are free online groups sometimes referred to as "loops" where people post and share. With information from this book, you may join the online discussion groups at the emails or websites listed. Then you may post, and receive other people's posts and shares at your email address. You may join as many online discussion groups as you like. You may participate in as many discussion groups as you like. You may unsubscribe from the discussion group to stop receiving posts at any time you like.

What is a Sponsor?

A Sponsor is someone who will guide you to learn about yourself, your life issues, and your eating, by drawing on their own experience and answers. A Sponsor may help you by being available for daily contact to talk about food choices, eating, or life issues. A Sponsor may help you to give up a certain food substance, trigger food, or avoid certain foods, or plan shopping and eating. A Sponsor may help you through their experience and the writings of others.

What are Types of Sponsors?

Working with a Sponsor is one way for "one compulsive eater to help another." There are many ways to give and receive help.

There are Food Sponsors, Step Sponsors, E-Mail Sponsors, Maintenance Sponsors, Phone Group Sponsors, and Sponsors who recommend using cups and scales and weighing & measuring Food. Typically a Food Sponsor helps someone with their food choices daily. Some, but not all, Food Sponsors require that their Sponsees write down their food ahead of time and call it in. For some people this action is helpful and for others it isn't.

Sponsors from circles, such as the OA H.O.W. meetings, CEA-H.O.W, and Food Addicts Anonymous, have directions regarding food plan, weighing and measuring, attending meetings and making outreach calls. These are requirements for their Sponsees to follow.

It is up to you to decide if you want to work with someone who volunteers and you ask to Sponsor you. It is up to you to decide what you might want someone to help you with. The Sponsee usually works out with the Sponsor what the nature of the Sponsor-Sponsee contact will be. There are Sponsors you may talk with daily. There are Sponsors you may talk with on an as-needed basis about the 12 Steps or life issues.

Sponsors are individuals, individual human beings. There is no standard Sponsor.

How Do I Get a Sponsor – Be a Sponsee

In the "Sponsor-Phone Buddy" section you will learn more about the types of Sponsors available. You will learn how to get a Sponsor or list of Sponsors from the resource, and how to reach out to call and ask someone to Sponsor you.

Typically, you call someone to ask them to Sponsor you. They volunteer to be a Sponsor on a phone meeting, at a face-to-face meeting, in an online discussion group, or on a contact list. It's a two-way street. You may be helping someone who has volunteered to sponsor you more than you know.

It is in the reaching out that people get the confidence to talk about themselves and their eating. It is in the sponsoring that people get a confidence that they do know something and can help.

What is a Phone Buddy? What is an Action Partner?

How Do I Get a Phone Buddy or Action Partner

A Phone Buddy or Action Partner is someone who volunteers. When someone shares their contact information, phone number or email in a phone meeting, online meeting, at a face-to-face meeting, or in an online discussion group, they are available to talk.

A Phone Buddy or Action Partner may help you with daily or moment-by-moment contact when you are making food choices or taking other actions. They may help you define a plan of eating, or take other actions related to your life issues.

A Phone Buddy or Action Partner might be willing to let you "bookend" actions -- make a call before you create your shopping list and after you have completed your shopping list; make a call before you go grocery shopping and when you get home from grocery shopping; make a call before a meal and after a meal; make a call when around a dangerous food neighborhood or in a troublesome situation; make a call to a prospective employer or business contact, so you don't procrastinate or eat over it or get excessive anxiety, and close the "bookend" by making a phone call to the Phone Buddy or Action Partner when you have completed the difficult phone call or action.

How Is this Guide Organized?

We recommend that you read "Organizations" first to get an overview. This will give you a clear feeling for the organization's perspective and the type of resources available. Groups are listed in the date order in which the various circles and spinoffs were formed.

Then we recommend that you search the type of resource you might like to tap into:

ONLINE MEETING HELP
PHONE MEETING HELP
FACE-TO-FACE MEETING HELP
SPONSOR & PHONE BUDDY HELP
EMAIL RESOURCES - ONLINE DISCUSSION GROUPS
LITERATURE
ORGANIZATIONS

No one resource is recommended over another. You can familiarize yourself with the types of resources and approaches. Get to know them. Learn from them all. Use them.

There is wisdom on the wires. Learning how to do life one day at a time comes with being honest and open with at least one other human being. We are not all weak in the same spots or at the same time.

We hope you enjoy this book. It is not meant to be a complete guide to each group or circle - merely a beginning to get you started. We hope it reaches a wide public.

Overeaters Anonymous Inc. (OA)

http://www.oa.org
PO Box 44020
Rio Rancho, New Mexico 87174-4020 USA
http://www.oa.org/contact.php
505-891-2664

Are there online meetings?
- Yes

How do I get a list of online meetings?
- Click on: http://www.oa.org/pdfs/onlinemeetingslist.pdf
  for a pdf Printed List of Online Meetings
- Go to: http://www.oa.org/meetings/find-a-meeting-online.php
  for a complete list of OA Online Meetings
- Go to http://www.therecoverygroup.org/newcomers.html and click the
  doorway, to see OA meetings registered with OA World Services, or
  Go to: http://www.therecoverygroup.org/meetings/index.html.
- Go to: http://oa12step4coes.org for a list of online meeting times and days,
  for online OA meetings sponsored by this OA Intergroup.
  Login at: http://www.irc.starchat.net
- Online OA meetings are held by • Overeaters Anonymous Inc. • The Recovery
  Group • OA12StepforCOES at website addresses.   The Online meetings take
  place through Online Chat or Online SKYPE telephone. The meetings follow
  a meeting format. The Recovery Group online meetings are not affiliated with
  Overeaters Anonymous Inc. The OA endorsed online meetings are registered
  on http://www.oa.org/meetings/find-a-meeting-online.php

What are the types of online meetings?
- AA Big Book
- Beginner/Newcomer
- Hebrew
- Italian
- OA H.O.W.
- Spanish
- 12 Steps & 12 Traditions

CEA-HOW (Compulsive Overeaters Anonymous-HOW)

http://www.ceahow.org/
5500 E. Atherton St., Suite 227-B
Long Beach, CA 90815-4017
562-342-9344
CEA-HOW General Service Office: gso@ceahow

Are there online meetings?
- No

Food Addicts Anonymous, Inc.

http://www.foodaddictsanonymous.org/meetings-events
561-967-3871

Are there online meetings?
- Yes

How do I get a list of online meetings?
- Go to: http://www.foodaddictsanonymous.org/meetings-events

What are the types of online meetings?
- Phone Meeting and Chat Room On-Line Meetings
Nationwide Meetings for FAA on the Web
- If you have Netscape or MS Internet Explorer, you can attend live FAA meetings in the FAA Chatroom. If you have AOL, you can also participate in the meetings.
- Meeting Days and Times
<u>FAA On-Line Regular Meetings</u>
Sundays 1pm EST and 10am PST
<u>FAA On-Line Beginners Meeting</u>
Saturday 11am EST and 8am PST

The Recovery Group

http://www.therecoverygroup.org/

Are there online meetings?
- Yes

What are the types of online meetings?
- AA Big Book
- Beginner/Newcomer
- Hebrew
- Italian
- OA H.O.W.
- Spanish
- 12 Steps & 12 Traditions

Greysheeters Anonymous (GSA)

http://www.greysheet.org/cms/
GSA World Services or GSAWS, Inc.
Cherokee Station
PO Box 20098
New York, NY 10021-0061
uscontacts@greysheet.org
phonelist@greysheet.org

Are there online meetings?
- No

Food Addiction: The Body Knows

http://www.kaysheppard.com/
kshepp825@aol.com
321-727-8040

Are there online meetings?
- Yes

How do I get a list of online meetings?
- Go to: http://www.kaysheppard.com/chat.htm

What are the types of online meetings?
- **Monday: 9:00 p.m. EST: Chat Room:**
  http://www.kaysheppard.com/chat.htm
- **Wednesday: 7:00 p.m. EST: Chat Room:**
  http://www.kaysheppard.com/chat.htm
- **Sunday: 8 p.m. EST: Chat Room:**
  http://www.kaysheppard.com/chat.htm

Anorexics & Bulimics Anonymous

http://www.anorexicsandbulimicsanonymousaba.com/
Main P.O. Box 125 | Edmonton, AB T5J 2G9
780-443-6077

Are there online meetings?
- No

12 Steps for Compulsive Overeaters (OA12StepsforCOES)
Online 12 Step Group for Compulsive Overeaters

OA Inc. Registered Intergroup
http://www.oa12step4coes.org
sunlight@oa12step4coes.org

Are there online meetings?
- Yes

How do I get a list of online meetings?
- **To Get Started: Meetings 7 Days a Week at: 7:00 a.m., 10:30 a.m., 2:30 p.m., 6:00 p.m., 8:15 p.m., 10:30 p.m., 12:30 a.m.**
- **Click on:** http://www.starchat.net/chat/index.php?chan=12step4coes
- **Go to:** http://www.oa12step4coes.org/meetings.html **for a list of meetings**
- **Click on the Chat Room.**

What are the types of online meetings?
- **Chat room:**
- **12 Step 4 Compulsive Overeaters:**
  http://www.oa12step4coes.org/loops/esh.html
- **Abstinent 4 Today:**
  http://www.oa12step4coes.org/loops/abstinent.html
- **12 Step 4 Today:**
  http://www.oa12step4coes.org/loops/today.html
- **12 Step 4 Mom Compulsive Overeaters:**
  http://www.oa12step4coes.org/loops/mom.html
- **12 Step 4 Male Compulsive Overeaters:**
  http://www.oa12step4coes.org/loops/male.html
- **12 Step 4 Senior Spirit Compulsive Overeaters:**
  http://www.oa12step4coes.org/loops/senior.html
- **12 Step 4 Teen Compulsive Overeaters:**
  http://www.oa12step4coes.org/loops/teen.html
- **12 Step 4 Compulsive Overeaters Food Talk:**
  http://www.oa12step4coes.org/loops/foodtalk.html

Recovery from Food Addiction (RFA)

http://health.groups.yahoo.com/group/recoveryfromfoodaddiction/
recoveryfromfoodaddiction-subscribe@yahoogroups.com
P.O. Box 35543
713-673-2848

Are there online meetings?
- No

OA Primary Purpose

http://www.oapp.info/oaprimarypurposegroups
http://health.groups.yahoo.com/group/oapp/links
oapp-subscribe@yahoogroups.com

Are there online meetings:
- No

The Coffee Shop

712-432-3900 Access PIN: 897578#
Daily - 7 A.M. EST
Recorded meeting:
712-432-3903 Access PIN: 897578#
Press 0# for most recent recording

Are there online meetings:
- No

The Parking Lot

712-432-3900
Access PIN: 6508933#
Daily - 1 A.M. - 6:30 A.M. EST

Are there online meetings:
- No

Cups & Scales

http://groups.yahoo.com/group/cupsscalesgroup
cupsscalesgroup-subscribe@yahoogroups.com

Are there online meetings:

- No

Overeaters Anonymous Inc. (OA)

http://www.oa.org
PO Box 44020
Rio Rancho, New Mexico 87174-4020 USA
http://www.oa.org/contact.php
505-891-2664

Are there phone meetings?
- Yes

How do I get a list of phone meetings?
- To Get Started: Phone Meetings
-
   Daily: 6.45 a.m., 6:45 p.m., 9 p.m. EST:
   Phone Number: 712-432-3900 PIN: 4285115#
- Monday-Friday: 12 NOON EST.:
   Phone Number: 712-432-3900 PIN: 915892#
- Daily: 10, p.m., 11 p.m., 12 Midnight, EST.:
   Phone Number: 712-432-3900 PIN: 936221#
- Daily: 12 Midnight EST:
   Phone Number: 712-432-3900 PIN: 6508933#
   Figure the meeting time at your time zone.
- Click on http://www.oa.org/pdfs/phone_mtgs.pdf
   for a Printed List of OA Phone Meetings"
- Go to http://www.oa.org. Click on Meetings.
   Click on Telephone. Set your Time Zone; Print Phone Meeting List
- If you do not have a computer to get a phone meeting list
   Call Deb at 503-720-6157
   She will send you a phone meeting list by mail.
- Over 150 OA Phone Meetings a Week

What are the types of phone meetings?
- *AA 12 Step Steps & Traditions* - Focuses on reading from the AA 12 Steps &
   Traditions and discussing each step and tradition in relation to compulsive
   eating.
- Anorexia-Bulemia - Focuses on starving, restricting, purging and diet
   remedies as compulsive behaviors to deal with compulsive eating.
- Beginner/Newcomer - Focuses on an introduction to the Steps & Traditions
   and Tools of OA for the Newcomer; how to get a Sponsor, Phone Buddy or
   Action Partner, and OA resources.

- Big Book - Focuses on reading and discussing *The AA Big Book*.

- Black - Focuses on being black with reference to compulsive eating & OA; open to everyone.
- *For Today* - Literature passages, reading and discussion from the *OA For Today* book of Meditations.
- *Lifeline* - Literature passages, reading and discussion from the *OA Lifeline Magazine*, current and back issues.
- Literature Study - Literature passages, reading and discussion from OA and AA-approved literature.
- Meditations - Literature readings, meditations, sharing on meditations.
- Men's - Discussion and sharing related to men.
- 90 Day* - Meetings giving help to people who want a structured approach, including weighing and measuring, calling a Sponsor daily, making three outreach calls daily, and 90 days abstinence to share on phone meetings. To Get Started with a 90-day Meeting:
Monday 10 a.m.EST: Phone Number: 213-289-0500 PIN: 79822#
Tuesday 9:30 a.m. EST: Phone Number: 712-432-8773 PIN: 45698#
- *OA 12 Steps & Traditions*- Focuses on the OA 12 Steps & Traditions.
- OA H.O.W* - "H.O.W. is a movement within Overeaters Anonymous whose basic principle is that abstinence is the only means to freedom from compulsive overeating and the beginning of a spiritual life. We believe that the discipline of weighing and measuring, of telephoning your sponsor at a particular time, of attending meetings and making phone calls; all lead to a life based on the Universal Discipline, which is accord rather than discord even with many things going on around us. • We eat weighed and measured meals with nothing in between except sugar free beverages and sugar free gum. • Food is written down, called in to our sponsor and committed, so that we can get on with our recovery and out of the food. • We do not write our own food plan. We use a food plan given to us by a doctor, nutritionist or dietician. We discuss it with our sponsor. We do not pick one that allows any of our binge foods. If some food on our plan becomes a problem, we avoid it. • We do not skip meals, switch meals or combine eals. We do not deviate or manipulate our food plan in any way. If we need to change our committed food during the day, we call a sponsor. • We weigh and measure all our portions so that there is no guess work. We do not measure by eye. We use a measuring cup, spoon, and a scale. • We weigh ourselves once a month until we reach goal weight and once a week on maintenance. • Unless advised otherwise by your doctor, we take a multi-vitamin and drink 64 oz. of water a day. • We do not drink alcohol. • We do not use foods containing sugar, except if sugar is listed 5th or beyond on the ingredients label. • A H.O.W. sponsor is a compulsive overeater who has completed at least 70 days of

back-to-back
abstinence and who has taken the first three steps of the

program. Sponsors have also completed at least 70 days of assignments.
• In HOW we are asked to make at least 4 telephone calls a day; one to our sponsor and 3 more to other OA members. These calls give us an opportunity to "talk program" on a daily basis. • As H.O.W. members we attend at least one H.O.W. meeting a week." (OA H.O.W. Statement, March 2010).
To Get Started with a H.O.W. Meeting:
Monday 8:30 p.m. EST: Phone Number: 270-696-2525 PIN: 121208#
Tuesday 12:30 a.m. EST: Phone Number: 712-432-1436 PIN: 121208#
Tuesday: 100 Pounders-How: 6:45 p.m. EST:
Phone Number: 712-432-0075 PIN: 619342#

- One Hundred Pounders- 100 Pounders - Focuses on recovery for people who have lost or want to lose 100 pounds or more
- Relapse/Recovery *12th Step Within* - Literarure/discussion from *12th Step Within*
- *Seeking the Spiritual Path* - Literature/discussion on *Seeking the Spiritual Path*
- Speaker/Qualification - A Speaker will share his/her Experience, Strength, Hope on recovery.
- Topic/Discussion - Moderator will set a topic for discussion.
- *Voices of Recovery* - Literature/discussion *Voices of Recovery*
- Weighing & Measuring* - OA 90 Day and OA H.O.W. meetings suggest weighing and measuring food as part of a structured approach to being released from compulsive eating.
- Young People/Everyone - Topic/Discussion with Young People/Everyone

Are there all day phone marathons?
- Holiday Marathons: Phone Number: 712-432-3900 PIN: 4285115 from 6:45 a.m. EST to Midnight EST, Continuously Every Hour.
- OA Special Day Phone Marathons

How do I get a list of marathon phone meetings dates & times?
- Holiday Marathons: Phone Number: 712-432-3900 PIN: 4285115 from 6:45 a.m. EST to Midnight EST, Continuously Every Hour.
- Send a blank email to oaphonemarathons-subscribe@yahoogroups.com for a list of OA • Special Day Phone Marathons

CEA-HOW (Compulsive Overeaters Anonymous-HOW)

http://www.ceahow.org/
5500 E. Atherton St., Suite 227-B
Long Beach, CA 90815-4017
562-342-9344
CEA-HOW General Service Office: gso@ceahow

Are there phone meetings?
- Yes

How do I get a list of phone meetings?
- **To Get Started: Phone Meetings Daily: 5:30 a.m., 7 a.m., 10 a.m., 1 p.m.,4 p.m., 5 p.m., 7 p.m., 6:45 p.m., 9 p.m., 10:30 p.m., 11 p.m., 12 Midnight, EST. • Figure the meeting time at your time zone. • Phone Number: (712)-432-1680, access code: 152077#.**
- **Go to: http://www.ceahow-org?q=content/phone-bridge-meetings for a complete list of phone meetings**

- **How do I get a list of "We Care" phone numbers & email addresses, people willing to help?**
- **Click on: http://tinyurl.com/24kzgos for Phone Numbers & Email addresses for Phone Buddies, Action Partners & Sponsors, and to volunteer to be a Phone Buddy, Action Partner or Sponsor.**
- **Send an email to: phonebridgeoutreach@gmail.com for a list of Phone Numbers, Email addresses for Phone Buddies, Action Partners & Sponsors, and to volunteer to be a Phone Buddy, Action Partner or Sponsor.**

What are the types of phone meetings?
- 12 & 12
- *AA Big Book*
- *AA Comes of Age*
- *As Bill Sees It*
- *Came to Believe*
- *Daily Reflections*
- *Living Sober*
- **Promises**
- **Relapse Prevention**
- **Speaker Qualification**
- **Steps/Traditions**
- **The CEA-HOW Concept**

Food Addicts Anonymous, Inc.

http://www.foodaddictsanonymous.org/meetings-events
561-967-3871

Are there phone meetings?
- Yes

How do I get a list of phone meetings?
- Click on http://www.foodaddictsanonymous.org/meetings-events
- To get started, dial 712-451-6000 PIN 7393#
  Sunday - 8 a.m., 9 a.m, 6 p.m., 10:30 p.m. EST
  Monday - 5:45 a.m., 10 a.m., 7 p.m., 9 p.m. 10:30 p.m. EST
  Tuesday - 5:45 a.m., 3 p.m., 8 p.m., 10 p.m. EST
  Wednesday - 5:45 a.m., 7 a.m., 11 a.m., 6:30 p.m., 10 p.m. EST
  Thursday - 5:45 a.m., 3 p.m., 9 p.m. EST
  Friday - 5:45 a.m., 11 a.m., 8 p.m., 10 p.m. EST
  Saturday - 8 a.m., 10 a.m., 8 p.m. EST

What are the types of phone meetings?

- **Food for the Soul**
- **Newcomers**
- **Speaker**
- **Promises**
- **Tools**
- **Literature**

Are there all day phone marathons?
- No

The Recovery Group
http://www.therecoverygroup.org/

Are there phone meetings?
- Yes
- The Recovery Group has phone meetings, online meetings, online email discussion groups, and phone buddy, action partner, and sponsor services. The meetings follow a meeting format. The Recovery Group is not affiliated with Overeaters Anonymous Inc. The OA endorsed online meetings led by Recovery Group Moderators are registered on http://www.oa.org/meetings/find-a-meeting-online.php.
- Go to http://www.oa.org. Click on Meetings. Click on Telephone.
  Set your Time Zone;
  Print Phone Meeting List
- Send a blank email to: oaphonemeetings-subscribe@yahoogroups.com

What are the types of phone meetings?
- AA Big Book
- Beginner/Newcomer

Greysheeters Anonymous (GSA)

http://www.greysheet.org/cms/
GSA World Services or GSAWS, Inc.
Cherokee Station
PO Box 20098
New York, NY 10021-0061
uscontacts@greysheet.org
phonelist@greysheet.org

Are there phone meetings?
- Yes

How do I get a list of phone meetings?
- Go to: http://www.greysheet.org/cms/phone-meetings.html
- Send an email to: phonemeetings@greysheet.org for a list of phone meetings and PINS.

What are the types of phone meetings?
- *12 & 12*
- *AA Big Book*
- *AA Literature/Topic*
- *As Bill Sees It*
- Beginners
- Literature
- Living Sober
- Qualification/Speaker
- Relapse/Recovery
- Step Study

Are there all day phone marathons?
- No

Food Addiction: The Body Knows

http://www.kaysheppard.com/
kshepp825@aol.com
321-727-8040

Are there phone meetings?
- Yes

How do I get a list of phone meetings?
- To Get Started: Tuesday: 8 p.m. EST: Phone Number (712) 432-1100, PIN: 517590: "12 Steps & 12 Traditions of Alcoholics Anonymous" Discussion Thursday: 8 p.m. EST: Phone Number (712) 432-1100, PIN: 517590#: Topic: 12 Steps & 12 Traditions of Alcoholics Anonymous Saturday: 12 noon EST: Phone Number (712) 432-1100, PIN: 517590#: "From the First Bite" Discussion Sunday: 12 noon EST: Phone Number (712) 432-1100, PIN: 517590#: "The Big Book of Alcoholics Anonymous" Discussion

What are the types of phone meetings?
- *Alcoholics Anonymous, 4th ed.* Discussion
- *Alcoholics Anonymous 12 Steps & 12 Traditions* Discussion
- *From the First Bite* Discussion

Anorexics & Bulimics Anonymous

http://www.anorexicsandbulimicsanonymousaba.com/
Main P.O. Box 125 | Edmonton, AB T5J 2G9
780-443-6077

Are there phone meetings?
- Yes

How do I get a list of phone meetings?
- To Get Started: Monday 8:30 EST • Phone Number: 218-862-1403 PIN: 22657# ; Tuesday 2 p.m. • Phone Number: 213-289-0500 PIN: 22657#• Friday 11:30 a.m. • Phone Number: 213-289-0500 PIN: 22657#.
- Go to: http://tinyurl.com/28eqc5d for a list of meetings.

What are the types of phone meetings?
- Anorexics & Bulemics Anonymous

12 Steps for Compulsive Overeaters (OA12StepsforCOES)
Online 12 Step Group for Compulsive Overeaters

OA Inc. Registered Intergroup
http://www.oa12step4coes.org
sunlight@oa12step4coes.org

Are there phone meetings?
- No

Recovery from Food Addiction (RFA)

http://health.groups.yahoo.com/group/recoveryfromfoodaddiction/
recoveryfromfoodaddiction-subscribe@yahoogroups.com
P.O. Box 35543
713-673-2848

Are there phone meetings?
- Yes

How do I get a list of phone meetings?
- **To get started dial 218-339-4300 PIN 1086405#**
  Friday Night @ 9:00 pm EST

What are the types of phone meetings?
- **Recovery from Food Addiction**

Are there all day phone marathons?
- No

OA Primary Purpose

http://www.oapp.info/oaprimarypurposegroups
http://health.groups.yahoo.com/group/oapp/links
oapp-subscribe@yahoogroups.com
712-432-3900 PIN 643578#

Are there online SKYPE phone meetings?

- Yes

How do I get a list of the online SKYPE phone meetings?

- To get started send an email to the Host of the Skype Open Big Book Study Meetings to Request an Invitation: OAPP Coordinator: Joni P. at joni@oapp.info.
- You will receive an email back confirming you have been added to the Yahoogroups discussion group to receive the list of questions and answers each day.
- OAPP Skype Phone Meetings are held on the following days and times: Day USA/CST Speaker Host Program Host Monday 11:00 AM Cliff Bishop Joni B OA joni@oapp.info

The Coffee Shop

712-432-3900 Access PIN: 897578#
Daily - 7 A.M. EST
Recorded meeting:
712-432-3903 Access PIN: 897578#
Press 0# for most recent recording

Are there phone meetings:

- Yes

How do I get a list of phone meetings?

- Daily 7 a.m. EST
  To Get started: dial 712-432-3900 PIN: 897578#. To reach the most recent recorded meeting dial: 712-432-3903 PIN: 897578# and press 0#.

The Parking Lot

712-432-3900
Access PIN: 6508933#
Daily - 1 A.M. - 6:30 A.M. EST

Are there phone meetings?

* Yes

* Started in 2010, The Parking Lot is an all-night open phone discussion. It goes from 1 a.m. to 6:30 a.m. or later EST. You can adjust the times for your time zone. The discussion is not an official   meeting of any organization. It follows an open discussion format. There is a moderator. It is moderated by I Irene and others.
* People do readings, poetry, music, and open sharing. The discussion is for night-eaters, night workers, people who eat in the middle of the night, or people who want recovery. Other 12 step programs such as Debtors Anonymous, Clutters Anonymous, or others may be discussed. The emphasis is on recovery.
* People talk on topics such as daily struggles, insights, lessons, and anything related to recovery. The purpose is to save lives. People share phone numbers and emails to receive outreach calls.

Cups & Scales

http://groups.yahoo.com/group/cupsscalesgroup
cupsscalesgroup-subscribe@yahoogroups.com

Are there phone meetings:

* No

Overeaters Anonymous Inc. (OA)

http://www.oa.org
PO Box 44020
Rio Rancho, New Mexico 87174-4020 USA
http://www.oa.org/contact.php
505-891-2664

Are there face-to-face meetings?
- **Yes**

How do I get a list of face-to-face meetings?
- **Go to** http://www.oa.org
  Click on Meetings in Upper Righthand corner or Lefthand Navigation Bar; Click on Find a Face-to-Face Meeting; Click on your Location: Continent, State, City, Print Face-to-Face Meeting List for your Location.

- **In addition to the above resources, for meeting information in a specific area, we recommend that you contact your nearest OA Intergroup, search for a meeting on the OA World Service Office website** http://www.oa.org, **or contact Intergroups within each region to get lists of meetings under the Intergroup:**
- **OA Region 1: Intergroup Websites:** http://oaregion1.org/intergroups/intergroups.htm
  Alaska ~ Alberta ~ N.W. Territories ~ Saskatchewan ~ Yukon ~ British Columbia ~ Oregon ~ Washington ~ Idaho ~ Montana ~ Wyoming
- **OA Region 2: Intergroup Websites:** http://oaregion2.org
  California ~ Mexico ~ Hawaii ~ N. Nevada
- **OA Region 3: Intergroup Websites:** http://oaregion3.org/intergroups.html
  Arizona ~ Colorado ~ Southern Nevada ~ New Mexico ~ Oklahoma ~ Texas ~ Utah
- **OA Region 4: Intergroup Websites:** http://69.89.31.172/~oaregion/?cat=8
  Illinois [except the Chicagoland area] ~ Iowa ~ Kansas ~ Missouri ~ Minnesota ~ Nebraska ~ North Dakota ~ South Dakota ~ Manitoba ~ Northwest Ontario ~ and Nunavut Territory ~ Canada
- **OA Region 5: Intergroup Websites:** http://oaregion5.org
  Northern Illinois ~ Indiana ~ Kentucky ~ Michigan ~ Ohio ~ Southern Ontario ~ Wisconsin

- OA Region 6: Intergroup Websites: http://oaregion6.org/en/?page_id=7
  Connecticut ~ Massachusettes~ Maine ~ New Brunswick ~ New Hampshire ~
  New York ~ Newfoundland & Labrador ~ Novia Scotia ~ Ontario ~ Quebec ~
  Rhode Island ~ Vermont ~ Francais
- OA Region 7: Intergroup Websites: http://oaregion7.org/intergroups/
  Delaware ~ Maryland ~ New Jersey ~ Pennsylvania ~ Virginia ~ Washington, DC
  ~ West Virginia
- OA Region 8: Intergroup Websites:
  http://oaregion8.org/meetings/meeting-list/
  Alabama ~ Arkansas ~ Florida ~ Georgia ~ Louisiana ~ Mississippi ~ North
  Carolina~ Puerto Rico ~ South Carolina ~ Tennessee.
  Countries:
  Brazil ~ Brazil NSB ~ Columbia ~ Columbia NSB ~ Costa Rica ~ Cuba ~
  Guatamala
- OA Region 9: Intergroup Websites:
  Africa, Europe, Middle East, Western Asia
  Austria: http://www.overeatersanonymous.at/
  Belgium: http://www.anoniemeovereters.be/
  Finland: http://www.oafinland.org/
  France: http://oainfos.org/
  Germany: http://www.overeatersanonymous.de/
  Great Britain: http://www.oagb.org.uk/
  Greece: http://anonymoi-yperfagoi.weebly.com/
  Island: http://www.oa.is/
  Israel: http://www.oa-israel.org/
  Italy: http://www.overeatersanonymous.it/go/
  Netherlands: http://www.anonieme-overeters.nl/
  Norway: http://www.overeatersanonymous.no/
  Poland: http://www.anonimowizarlocy.org/
  Slovenia: http://oa-slovenija.com/
  Sweden: http://www.oasverige.org/
  Spain: http://www.comedorescompulsivos.es/
- OA Region 10: Intergroup Websites: http://www.oaregion10.org/links.html
  Australia, New Zealand, Japan, South East Asia, Western Pacific Basin

What are the types of face-to-face meetings?

- **AA 12 Step Steps & Traditions** - Focuses on reading from the AA 12 Steps & Traditions and discussing each step and tradition in relation to compulsive eating.
- **Anorexia-Bulemia** - Focuses on starving, restricting, purging and diet remedies as compulsive behaviors to deal with compulsive eating.
- **Beginner/Newcomer** - Focuses on an introduction to the Steps & Traditions and Tools of OA for the Newcomer; how to get a Sponsor, Phone Buddy or Action Partner, and OA resources.
- **Big Book** - Focuses on reading and discussing The AA Big Book with reference to compulsive eating.
- **Black** - Focuses on being black with reference to compulsive eating & OA; open to everyone.
- **Discussion - AA** - Focuses on Alcoholics Anonymous literature with reference to being a compulsive eater.
- **For Today** - Literature passages, reading and discussion from the OA For Today book of Meditations.
- **Lifeline** - Literature passages, reading and discussion from the OA Lifeline Magazine, current and back issues.
- **Literature Study** - Literature passages, reading and discussion from OA and AA-approved literature.
- **Meditations** - Literature readings, meditations, sharing on meditations.
- **Men's** - Discussion and sharing related to men.
- **90 Day*** - Meetings giving help to people who want a structured approach, including weighing and measuring, calling a Sponsor daily, making three outreach calls daily, and 90 days abstinence to share on phone meetings.
- **OA 12 Steps & Traditions**- Focuses on the OA 12 Steps & Traditions.
- **OA H.O.W*** - "H.O.W. is a movement within Overeaters Anonymous whose basic principle is that abstinence is the only means to freedom from compulsive overeating and the beginning of a spiritual life. We believe that the discipline of weighing and measuring, of telephoning your sponsor at a particular time, of attending meetings and making phone calls; all lead to a life based on the Universal Discipline, which is accord rather than discord even with many things going on around us. • We eat weighed and measured meals with nothing in between except sugar free beverages and sugar free gum. • Food is written down, called in to our sponsor and committed, so that we can get on with our recovery and out of the food. • We do not write our own food plan. We use a food plan given to us by a doctor, nutritionist or dietician. We discuss it with our sponsor. We do not pick one that allows any of our binge foods. If some food on our plan becomes a problem, we avoid it. • We do not skip meals, switch meals or combine meals. We do not deviate or

CEA-HOW (Compulsive Overeaters Anonymous-HOW)

http://www.ceahow.org/
5500 E. Atherton St., Suite 227-B
Long Beach, CA 90815-4017
562-342-9344
CEA-HOW General Service Office: gso@ceahow

Are there face-to-face meetings?
- Yes

How do I get a list of face-to-face meetings?
- Click on: http://tinyurl.com/27aoofu for a list of Face-to-Face Meetings.

What are the types of face-to-face meetings?
- 12 & 12
- AA Big Book
- AA Comes of Age
- As Bill Sees It
- Came to Believe
- Daily Reflections
- Living Sober
- Promises
- Relapse Prevention
- Speaker Qualification
- Steps/Traditions
- The CEA-HOW Concept
- Topic Discussion

Food Addicts Anonymous, Inc.

http://www.foodaddictsanonymous.org/meetings-events
561-967-3871

Are there face-to-face meetings?
- Yes

How do I get a list of face-to-face meetings?
- Click on: http://www.foodaddictsanonymous.org/meetings-events

What are the Types of face-to-face meetings?
- Face to face, two or more compulsive overeaters come together to share.

Greysheeters Anonymous (GSA)

http://www.greysheet.org/cms/
GSA World Services or GSAWS, Inc.
Cherokee Station
PO Box 20098
New York, NY 10021-0061
uscontacts@greysheet.org
phonelist@greysheet.org

Are there face-to-face meetings?
- Yes

How do I get a list of face-to-face meetings?
- Go to: http://www.greysheet.org/cms/face-to-face-meetings.html

What are the types of face-to-face meetings?
- *12 & 12*
- *AA Big Book*
- *AA Literature/Topic*
- *As Bill Sees It*
- Beginners
- Literature
- Living Sober
- Men's Meeting
- Qualification/Speaker
- Relapse/Recovery
- Step Study

Food Addiction: The Body Knows

http://www.kaysheppard.com/
kshepp825@aol.com
321-727-8040

Are there face-to-face meetings?
- Yes

How do I get a list of face-to-face meetings?
- Go to: http://www.kaysheppard.com

What are the Types of face-to-face meetings?
- Food Addiction: The Body Knows

Anorexics & Bulimics Anonymous

http://www.anorexicsandbulimicsanonymousaba.com/
Main P.O. Box 125 | Edmonton, AB T5J 2G9
780-443-6077

Are there face-to-face meetings?
- Yes

How do I get a list of face-to-face meetings?
- Go to: http://www.anorexicsandbulimicsanonymousaba.com/
- Click on Meetings.
- Go to: http://tinyurl.com/28eqc5d for a list of **meetings.**

What are the Types of face-to-face meetings?
- Anorexics & Bulemics Anonymous

12 Steps for Compulsive Overeaters (OA12StepsforCOES)
Online 12 Step Group for Compulsive Overeaters

> OA Inc. Registered Intergroup
> http://www.oa12step4coes.org
> sunlight@oa12step4coes.org

Are there face-to-face meetings?
- No

Recovery from Food Addiction (RFA)

> http://health.groups.yahoo.com/group/recoveryfromfoodaddiction/
> recoveryfromfoodaddiction-subscribe@yahoogroups.com
> P.O. Box 35543
> 713-673-2848

Are there face-to-face meetings?
- Yes

How do I get a list of face-to-face meetings?
- To get these documents:
  Join the online discussion group Recovery from Food Addiction
  Send a blank email to:
  recoveryfromfoodaddiction-subscribe@yahoogroups.com
  After you have joined and received your confirmation, go to your yahoogroups:
  http://health.groups.yahoo.com/group/recoveryfromfoodaddiction/)."
  Go to your Group: Recovery from Food Addiction.
  Go to Files in the lefthand column on the homepage.
  You will find a list of face-to-face meetings.

What are the Types of face-to-face meetings?
- Recovery from Food Addiction

OA Primary Purpose

http://www.oapp.info/oaprimarypurposegroups
http://health.groups.yahoo.com/group/oapp/links
oapp-subscribe@yahoogroups.com
712-432-3900 PIN 643578#

Are there face-to-face meetings?
- **No**

The Coffee Shop

712-432-3900 Access PIN: 897578#
Daily - 7 A.M. EST
Recorded meeting:
712-432-3903 Access PIN: 897578#
Press 0# for most recent recording

Are there face-to-face meetings?
- **No**

The Parking Lot

712-432-3900
Access PIN: 6508933#
Daily - 1 A.M. - 6:30 A.M. EST

Are there face-to-face meetings?
- **No**

Cups & Scales

http://groups.yahoo.com/group/cupsscalesgroup
cupsscalesgroup-subscribe@yahoogroups.com

Are there face-to-face meetings:
- **No**

Overeaters Anonymous Inc. (OA)

http://www.oa.org
PO Box 44020
Rio Rancho, New Mexico 87174-4020 USA
http://www.oa.org/contact.php
505-891-2664

Are there sponsors, phone buddies & action partners?
- Yes

How do I get a sponsor, phone buddy or action partner?
How do I get a list of "We Care" phone numbers & email addresses, people willing to help?

- Sponsors, Phone Buddies & Action Partners are available at: • Face-To-Face Meetings, • Phone Meetings, •Online Meetings • From "We Care" Phone Number & Email lists • By eMail or Mail.
- The "We Care" list is a list of people who have shared their phone numbers or emails to receive and give OA outreach contact. • Ask if the meeting has a "We Care" list. • Look at the "We Care" list and write down names and numbers. • Email for the "We Care" list at the email addresses given. Ask at a Phone Meeting, Face-to-Face Meeting, Online Meeting or Email Discussion Group for a Sponsor, Phone Buddy or Action Partner.
- Send a blank email to: oa645business-subscribe@yahoogroups.com to join. Once you have joined, go to the group at: http://health.groups.yahoo.com/group/oa645business/. Click on Files. You will see a PDF list of Phone Numbers & Email addresses, for Phone Buddies, Action Partners & Sponsors, and to volunteer to be a Phone Buddy, Action Partner or Sponsor from the 6:45 a.m. Sunrise Meeting.
- Send an email to: recoveryinaction@yahoo.com for a list of Phone Numbers & Email addresses, for Phone Buddies, Action Partners & Sponsors, and to volunteer to be a Phone Buddy, Action Partner or Sponsor from the OA H.O.W meeting.
- Send an email to: fortodaylunchtimemeeting@gmail.com for a list of Phone Numbers & Email addresses for Phone Buddies, Action Partners & Sponsors, and to volunteer to be a Phone Buddy, Action Partner or Sponsor from 12:00 Lunchtime meeting EST.
- Send an email to: pianosheila@yahoo.com or call Sheila P. at (303) 980-1664 for a list of Phone Numbers & Email addresses for Phone Buddies, Action Partners & Sponsors, and to volunteer to be a Phone Buddy, Action Partner or Sponsor from the 8:30 a.m. OA 90-Day Program

- Send an email to 100pounders@gmail for a list of Phone Numbers & Email addresses for Phone Buddies, Action Partners & Sponsors and to volunteer for outreach from the 100 Pounders meeting.
- **Send an email to: Sponsors@TheRecoveryGroup.org for a list Phone Numbers & Email addresses for Phone Buddies, Action Partners & Sponsors, and to volunteer to be a Phone Buddy, Action Partner or Sponsor from The Recovery Group - OA . Read about The Recovery Group Sponsor Program at: http://www.therecoverygroup.org/sponsors.html.**

- **Are you a Loner? Phone Buddies, Action Partners & Sponsors are available for Loners. Are you living in a remote area, away from nearby 12 Step meetings?**
- **Click http://www.oaregion10.org/PDFs/loners.pdf for some loner OA member outreach stories - Loner Stories.**
- **Click http://www.oa.org and complete the online form: http://www.oa.org/ pdfs/sbm_form.pdf for the OA World Service Office by Mail program, or email the World Service Office at info@oa.org. for support by mail or email. Or write directly to OA at: OA, PO Box 44020, Rio Rancho, NM 87174-4020 USA. Or identify your Region (see Regions below for U.S. States and Countries in regions 1-10).**

- **Email for a Phone Buddy, Action Partner or Sponsor at:**
  info@oaregion1.org
  info@oaregion2.org
  info@oaregion3.org
  info@oaregion4.org
  info@oaregion5.org
  info@oaregion6.org
  info@oaregion7.org
  info@oaregion8.org
  info@oaregion9.org
  info@oaregion10.org

What are the types of sponsors, phone buddies & action partners?
- **AA Big Book & 12 Steps Sponsor: Sponsors people who want to work through the AA Big Book and 12 Steps & 12 Traditions, by reading and discussing the materials, one-on-one.**
- **eMail Sponsor - Sponsors people who want to maintain an e-mail connection, writing to the sponsor on a regular basis, either their food food or ways they are working a program.**

- Food Sponsor: Sponsors people who want to discuss their food as a part of a personal plan of recovery.
- Inventory Sponsor: Sponsors people who want to read and learn about doing a Fourth Step Inventory, from various 4th Step materials, and to do the Inventory with a Sponsor, one-on-one.
- Maintenance Sponsor: Sponsors people who are working a personal plan of recovery and want to maintain their recovery.
- 90-Day Meeting Sponsor - Sponsors people who are working the 90 Day Program. The 90-Day program recommends weighing & measuring food from a plan of eating as part of a personal plan of recovery & making outreach phone calls. Attend a 90-Day Phone Meeting to listen to the suggestions advised in the 90-Day program and to get a 90-Day Meeting Sponsor.
- OA H.O.W. Sponsor - "A H.O.W. sponsor is a compulsive overeater who has completed at least 70 days of back-to-back abstinence and who has taken the first three steps of the program. Sponsors have also completed at least 70 days of assignments. • In HOW we are asked to make at least 4 telephone calls a day; one to our sponsor and 3 more to other OA members. These calls give us an opportunity to "talk program" on a daily basis. • As H.O.W. members we attend at least one H.O.W. meeting a week. H.O.W. is a movement within Overeaters Anonymous whose basic principle is that abstinence is the only means to freedom from compulsive overeating and the beginning of a spiritual life. We believe that the discipline of weighing and measuring, of telephoning your sponsor at a particular time, of attending meetings and making phone calls; all lead to a life based on the Universal Discipline, which is accord rather than discord even with many things going on around us. • We eat weighed and measured meals with nothing in between except sugar free beverages and sugar free gum. • Food is written down, called in to our sponsor and committed, so that we can get on with our recovery and out of the food. • We do not write our own food plan. We use a food plan given to us by- a doctor, nutritionist or dietician. We discuss it with our sponsor. We do not pick one that allows any of our binge foods. If some food on our plan becomes a problem, we avoid it. • We do not skip meals, switch meals or combine meals. We do not deviate or manipulate our food plan in any way. If we need to change our committed food during the day, we call a sponsor. • We weigh and measure all our portions so that there is no guess work. We do not measure by eye. We use a measuring cup, spoon, and a scale. • We weigh ourselves once a month until we reach goal weight and once a week on maintenance. • Unless advised otherwise by your doctor, we take a multi-vitamin and drink 64 oz. of water a day. • We do not drink alcohol. • We do not use foods containing sugar, except if sugar is listed 5th

or beyond on the ingredients label. Attend an OA-H.O.W. Phone Meeting or Face-to-Face Meeting to listen to the suggestions advised in the OA H.O.W. program, and to get an OA H.O.W. Sponsor(OA H.O.W. Statement, March 2010).

- Physical~Emotional~Spiritual - Threefold Sponsor - Sponsors people who want to work a three fold recovery for compulsive eating, physical, emotional, spiritual.
- Step Sponsor: Sponsors people who want to read about, discuss, and work though the practice of The Twelve Steps & Twelve Traditions with a Sponsor.
- Weighing & Measuring Sponsor - Sponsors people who want to use cups & scales to weigh & measure food from a food plan. Weighing & Measuring Sponsors are available by attending OA 90-Day and OA H.O.W. phone meetings, face-to-face meetings, and other phone meetings, and asking for a Sponsor who will Sponsor people who want to weigh and measure their food portions. On OA 90-Day, OA H.O.W. and many other meetings, people share about using weighing and measuring as part of their personal plan of recovery, and volunteer to help people get started weighing and measuring from a plan of eating.
- Phone Buddy: A Phone Buddy is a person who volunteers to give and receive phone calls to discuss a plan of action, plan of eating, daily food and live issues, as a method to achieve release from compulsive eating and solve other life issues.
- Action Partner: An Action Partner volunteers to develop and discuss a plan of action as a tool to move toward release from compulsive eating and to move beyond compulsive eating to address life issues.
- Friendship: Many friendships are formed as one compulsive eater helps another.

☺

CEA-HOW (Compulsive Overeaters Anonymous-HOW)

http://www.ceahow.org/
5500 E. Atherton St., Suite 227-B
Long Beach, CA 90815-4017
562-342-9344
CEA-HOW General Service Office: gso@ceahow

Are there sponsors, phone buddies & action partners?
- Yes

How do I get a sponsor, phone buddy or action partner?
How do I get a list of "We Care" phone numbers & email addresses, people available for outreach?
- Click on: http://tinyurl.com/24kzgos for Phone Numbers & Email addresses for Phone Buddies, Action Partners & Sponsors, and to volunteer to be a Phone Buddy, Action Partner or Sponsor.
- Send an email to: phonebridgeoutreach@gmail.com for a list of Phone Numbers, Email addresses for Phone Buddies, Action Partners & Sponsors, and to volunteer to be a Phone Buddy, Action Partner or Sponsor.
- Send an email to: phonebridgeoutreach@gmail.com for a list of Phone Numbers, Email addresses for Phone Buddies, Action Partners & Sponsors, and to volunteer to be a Phone Buddy, Action Partner or Sponsor.

What are the types of sponsors?
- **Food Sponsor:** Sponsors people who want to follow the requirements of the CEA-HOW method of refraining from compulsive eating.
- **Inventory Sponsor:** Sponsors people who want to read and learn about doing a Fourth Step Inventory, from various 4th Step materials, and to do the Inventory with a Sponsor, one-on-one.
- **Step Sponsor:** Sponsors people who want to read about discuss, and work though the practice of The Twelve Steps & Twelve Traditions with a Sponsor, one-on-one.
- **Maintenance Sponsor:** Sponsors people who are working a personal plan of recovery and want to maintain their recovery.
- **Threefold Sponsor:** Food, Inventory, Step, Maintenance: Physical, Emotional, Spiritual

☺

Food Addicts Anonymous, Inc.

http://www.foodaddictsanonymous.org/meetings-events
561-967-3871

Are there sponsors, phone buddies & action partners?
- Yes

How do I get a sponsor, phone buddy or action partner?
How do I get a list of "We Care" phone numbers & email addresses, people willing to help?
- Ask for a Sponsor, Phone Buddy or Action Partner in FAA.org.
- Send a blank email to: FAA-Loop-subscribe@yahoogroups.com or
- Click on http://groups.yahoo.com/group/FAALoop

What are the types of sponsors, phone buddies & action partners?
- Threefold Sponsor: Food, Inventory, Step, Maintenance: Physical, Emotional, Spiritual.

The Recovery Group
http://www.therecoverygroup.org/

Are there sponsors, phone buddies & action partners?
- Yes

How do I get a sponsor, phone buddy or action partner?
How do I get a list of "We Care" phone numbers & email addresses, people willing to help?
- Send an email to: Sponsors@TheRecoveryGroup.org for Phone Numbers & Email addresses for Phone Buddies, Action Partners & Sponsors, and to volunteer to be a Phone Buddy, Action Partner or Sponsor.
  Read about The Recovery Group Sponsor Program at:
  http://www.therecoverygroup.org/sponsors.html.
- Go to: http://www.therecoverygroup.org/sponsors.html

What are the types of sponsors?
- **Food Sponsor:** Sponsors people who want to discuss their food as a part of a personal plan of recovery.
- **Greysheet Food Plan Sponsor:** Sponsors people who want to discuss the • Greysheet Food Plan and their food. These Sponsors may or may not be members of Greysheeters Anonymous Inc.
- **Inventory Sponsor:** Sponsors people who want to read and learn about doing a Fourth Step Inventory, from various 4th Step materials, and to do the Inventory with a Sponsor.
- **Maintenance Sponsor:** Sponsors people who are working a personal plan of recovery and want to maintain their recovery.
- **Step Sponsor:** Sponsors people who want to read about discuss, and work through the practice of The Twelve Steps & Twelve Traditions with a Sponsor, one-on-one.
- **Weighing & Measuring Sponsor:** Sponsors people who want to use cups & scales to weigh & measure food from a plan of eating as part of a personal plan of recovery. Many people share about using weighing and measuring as part of their personal plan of recovery, and volunteer to help people get started weighing and measuring from a plan of eating in many meetings.
- **Threefold Sponsor:** Food, Inventory, Step, Maintenance: Physical, Emotional, Spiritual

Greysheeters Anonymous (GSA)

http://www.greysheet.org/cms/
GSA World Services or GSAWS, Inc.
Cherokee Station
PO Box 20098
New York, NY 10021-0061
uscontacts@greysheet.org
phonelist@greysheet.org

Are there sponsors, phone buddies & action partners?
- **Yes**

How do I get a sponsor, phone buddy or action partner?
How do I get a list of "We Care" phone numbers & email addresses, people willing to help?
- Subscribe to this monthly list publication at:
  http://www.greysheet.org/cms/international-contacts.html, which lists
  hundreds of members worldwide, including available sponsors.
- Sponsors are available at: • Face-To-Face Meetings, • Phone Meetings, • Online
  - For initial contact only, to obtain a sponsor's phone number, • International
  Phone List.
- Join GreyNet - Post a request to this online group, to obtain a sponsor's
  phone number privately.
- To subscribe to the greynet, send a blank email to:
  greynet-subscribe@yahoogroups.com.
- Join Online Greysheeters Anonymous Forums:
  http://www.greysheet.org/forum/.
- The "We Care" list is a list of people who have shared their phone numbers or
  emails to receive and give OA outreach contact. • Ask if the meeting has a
  "We Care" list. • Look at the "We Care" list and write down names and
  numbers. • Email for the "We Care" list at the email addresses given. Ask at
  a Phone Meeting, Face-to-Face Meeting, Online Meeting or Email Discussion
  Group for a Sponsor, Phone Buddy or Action Partner.
- Send an email to: phonelist@greysheet.org and
  uscontacts@greysheet.org
  for a list of Phone Numbers & Email addresses for Phone Buddies, Action
  Partners & Sponsors, and to volunteer to be a Phone Buddy, Action Partner
  or Sponsor. Provide your Name, Address, Phone Number(s), E-mail;
  Availability to Sponsor. The list will only be provided to people who supply
  information. Privary will be protected.

What are the types of sponsors, phone buddies & action partners?

- AA Big Book & 12 Steps Sponsor: Sponsors people who want to work through the AA Big Book and 12 Steps & 12 Traditions, by reading and discussing the materials, one-on-one.
- Food Sponsor: Sponsors people who want to discuss the Greysheet Food Plan and their food, weighing & measuring, and commit their food from the Greysheet before they eat it, to a Greysheet Sponsor, as a part of a personal plan of recovery.
- Inventory Sponsor: Sponsors people who want to read and learn about doing a Fourth Step Inventory, from various 4th Step materials, and to do the Inventory with a Sponsor, one-on-one.
- Maintenance Sponsor: Sponsors people who are working a personal plan of recovery and want to maintain their recovery.
- Step Sponsor: Sponsors people who want to read about, discuss, and work though the practice of The Twelve Steps & Twelve Traditions with a Sponsor, one-on-one.
- Weighing & Measuring Sponsor: Sponsors people who want to use cups & scales to weigh & measure food from a plan of eating as part of a personal plan of recovery. Many people share about using weighing and measuring as part of their personal plan of recovery, and volunteer to help people get started weighing and measuring from a plan of eating in many meetings.
- Threefold Sponsor: Food, Inventory, Step, Maintenance: Physical, Emotional, Spiritual.

☺

Food Addiction: The Body Knows

http://www.kaysheppard.com/
kshepp825@aol.com
321-727-8040

Are there sponsors, phone buddies & action partners?

- **Phone Buddies & Action Partners**

How do I get a phone buddy or action partner?

- **Send a blank email to:** thebodyknows-subscribe@yahoogroups.com **or**
  Click on http://health.groups.yahoo.com/group/TheBodyKnows/
- **Join the online discussion group.**
  Ask for a sponsor, phone buddy or action partner on the discussion group.
- **Kay Sheppard offers for fee counseling on the food plan she recommends:**
- **Send an email to:** kshepp825@aol.com

Sponsors
Phone Buddies

Anorexics & Bulimics Anonymous

http://www.anorexicsandbulimicsanonymousaba.com/
Main P.O. Box 125 | Edmonton, AB T5J 2G9
780-443-6077

Are there sponsors, phone buddies & action partners?
- Yes

How do I get a sponsor, phone buddy or action partner?
How do I get a list of "We Care" phone numbers & email addresses, people willing to help?
- To Get Started: Monday 8:30 EST • Phone Number: 218-862-1403 PIN: 22657# ; Tuesday 2 p.m. • Phone Number: 213-289-0500 PIN: 22657#• Friday 11:30 a.m. • Phone Number: 213-289-0500 PIN: 22657#.
- Go to: http://tinyurl.com/28eqc5d for a list of meetings.
- Go to a Phone Meeting for Face-to-Face Meetings. Ask for a phone buddy, action partner or sponsor.
- Ask if the meeting has a "We Care" list.

What are the types of sponsors, phone buddies & action partners?
- AA Big Book & 12 Steps Sponsor: Sponsors people who want to work through the AA Big Book and 12 Steps & 12 Traditions, by reading and discussing the materials, one-on-one.
- Food Sponsor: Sponsors people who want to discuss their food as a part of a personal plan of recovery.
- Inventory Sponsor: Sponsors people who want to read and learn about doing a Fourth Step Inventory, from various 4th Step materials, and to do the Inventory with a Sponsor, one-on-one.
- Maintenance Sponsor: Sponsors people who are working a personal plan of recovery and want to maintain their recovery. ·
- Step Sponsor: Sponsors people who want to read about discuss, and work though the practice of The Twelve Steps & Twelve Traditions with a Sponsor.
- Weighing & Measuring Sponsor: Sponsors people who want to use cups & scales to weigh & measure food from a plan of eating as part of a personal plan of recovery. Many people share about using weighing and measuring as part of their personal plan of recovery, and volunteer to help people get started weighing and measuring from a plan of eating in many meetings.
- Threefold Sponsor: Food, Inventory, Step, Maintenance: Physical, Emotional, Spiritual.

12 Steps for Compulsive Overeaters (OA12StepsforCOES)
Online 12 Step Group for Compulsive Overeaters
OA Inc. Registered Intergroup
http://www.oa12step4coes.org
sunlight@oa12step4coes.org

Are there sponsors, phone buddies & action partners?
- **Yes**

How do I get a sponsor, phone buddy or action partner?
How do I get a list of "We Care" phone numbers & email addresses, people willing to help?
- **Send an email to: sponsors@12step4coes.org for a list of Phone Numbers and Email addresses for Phone Buddies, Action Partners & Sponsors, and to volunteer to be a Phone Buddy, Action Partner or Sponsor. Phone Buddies, Action Partners and Sponsors are available from this list, from Online meetings, and Online email discussion groups.**
- **The "We Care" list is a list of people who have shared their phone numbers or emails to receive and give OA outreach contact. • Ask if the meeting has a "We Care" list. • Look at the "We Care" list and write down names and numbers. • Email for the "We Care" list at the email addresses given. • Ask for a Phone Buddy, Action Partner or Sponsor from the "We Care" list or at group meetings.**

What are the types of sponsors, phone buddies & action partners?
- **AA Big Book & 12 Steps Sponsor: Sponsors people who want to work through the AA Big Book and 12 Steps & 12 Traditions, by reading and discussing the materials, one-on-one.**
- **Food Sponsor: Sponsors people who want to discuss their food as a part of a personal plan of recovery.**
- **Inventory Sponsor: Sponsors people who want to read and learn about doing a Fourth Step Inventory, from various 4th Step materials, and to do the**
- **Inventory with a Sponsor, one-on-one.**
- **Maintenance Sponsor: Sponsors people who are working a personal plan of recovery and want to maintain their recovery.**
- **Step Sponsor: Sponsors people who want to read about discuss, and work though the practice of The Twelve Steps & Twelve Traditions with a Sponsor.**

(Side tab): Sponsors Phone Buddies

- **Weighing & Measuring Sponsor:** Sponsors people who want to use cups & scales to weigh & measure food from a plan of eating as part of a personal plan of recovery. Many people share about using weighing and measuring as part of their personal plan of recovery, and volunteer to help people get started weighing and measuring from a plan of eating in many meetings.
- **Threefold Sponsor: Food, Inventory, Step, Maintenance: Physical, Emotional, Spiritual**

☺

Recovery from Food Addiction (RFA)

http://health.groups.yahoo.com/group/recoveryfromfoodaddiction/
recoveryfromfoodaddiction-subscribe@yahoogroups.com
P.O. Box 35543
713-673-2848

Are there sponsors, phone buddies & action partners?
- Yes

How do I get a sponsor, phone buddy or action partner?
How do I get a list of "We Care" phone numbers & email addresses, people willing to p?
- Subscribe to: recoveryfromfoodaddiction-subscribe@yahoogroups.com for Phone Buddies, Action Partners & Sponsors, and to volunteer to be a Phone Buddy, Action Partner or Sponsor.

- Sponsors are available at meetings and from a "We Care" Phone Number and Email list, for a Sponsor, Phone Buddy, Action Partner or other form of help. Ask at a meeting for a Sponsor, Phone Buddy or Action Partner. Ask if a meeting has a "We Care" list. Look at the "We Care" list to see the individuals giving their Phone Number or Email contact information for outreach. Sponsors are available at: • Face-To-Face Meetings, • Phone Meetings, • From "We Care" Phone Number & Email lists

What are the types of sponsors, phone buddies & action partners?
- AA Big Book & 12 Steps Sponsor: Sponsors people who want to work through the AA Big Book and 12 Steps & 12 Traditions, by reading and discussing the materials.

OA Primary Purpose

> http://www.oapp.info/oaprimarypurposegroups
> http://health.groups.yahoo.com/group/oapp/links
> oapp-subscribe@yahoogroups.com
> 712-432-3900 PIN 643578#

Are there sponsors, phone buddies & action partners?
- Yes

How do I get a sponsor, phone buddy or action partner?
How do I get a list of "We Care" phone numbers & email addresses, people willing to help?
- Ask at a meeting for a Sponsor, Phone Buddy or Action Partner. Ask if a meeting has a "We Care" list. Look at the "We Care" list to see the individuals giving their Phone Number or Email contact information for outreach. Sponsors are available at: • Face-To-Face Meetings, • Phone Meetings, • From "We Care" Phone Number & Email lists

The Coffee Shop

> 712-432-3900 Access PIN: 897578#
> Daily - 7 A.M. EST
> Recorded meeting:
> 712-432-3903 Access PIN: 897578#
> Press 0# for most recent recording

Are there sponsors, phone buddies & action partners?
- Yes

How do I get a sponsor, phone buddy or action partner?
How do I get a list of "We Care" phone numbers & email addresses, people willing to help?
- Ask at a meeting for a Sponsor, Phone Buddy or Action Partner. Ask if a meeting has a "We Care" list.

The Parking Lot
Daily - 712-432-3900
Access PIN: 6508933#
1 A.M. - 6:30 A.M. EST

Are there sponsors, phone buddies & action partners?
- Yes

How do I get a sponsor, phone buddy or action partner?
How do I get a list of "We Care" phone numbers & email addresses, people willing to help?
- Ask at a discussion for a Sponsor, Phone Buddy or Action Partner.

Cups & Scales
http://groups.yahoo.com/group/cupsscalesgroup
cupsscalesgroup-subscribe@yahoogroups.com

Are there sponsors, phone buddies & action partners?
- Yes

How do I get a sponsor, phone buddy or action partner?
How do I get a list of "We Care" phone numbers & email addresses, people willing to help?
- Ask in a discussion group post for a Sponsor, Phone Buddy or Action Partner. Individuals give their Phone Number or Email contact information for outreach.

Overeaters Anonymous Inc. (OA)

> http://www.oa.org
> PO Box 44020
> Rio Rancho, New Mexico 87174-4020 USA
> http://www.oa.org/contact.php
> 505-891-2664

Are there online email discussion groups?
- **No**

How do I get a list of online email discussion groups?
- **Online OA & 12 Step Recovery email discussion groups are hosted by •
  OA12StepforCOES (an OA Intergroup) • The Recovery Group • OA Primary
  Purpose • Recovery from Food Addiction (RFA) • The Body Knows.**

Are there free meditations here?
- **No**

CEA-HOW (Compulsive Overeaters Anonymous-HOW)

http://www.ceahow.org/
5500 E. Atherton St., Suite 227-B
Long Beach, CA 90815-4017
562-342-9344
CEA-HOW General Service Office: gso@ceahow

Are there online email discussion groups?
- No

Does the organization have free meditations?
- No

Food Addicts Anonymous, Inc.

http://www.foodaddictsanonymous.org/meetings-events
561-967-3871

Are there online email discussion groups?
- Yes

How do I get a list of online email discussion groups?
- Click on http://greenfaa.nfshost.com/forum/
- Online OA & 12 Step Recovery email discussion groups are hosted by • OA12StepforCOES • The Recovery Group • Food Addicts Anonymous • OA Primary Purpose • Recovery from Food Addiction (RFA) • The Body Knows. People go to the Discussion Group's website address from their Internet and join the discussion group by using their individual email to post and receive messages. Individuals will receive emails from the discussion group at the individual's email address. People may post, discuss, and talk to other members in response to topics and discussion in the discussion group through email responses to discussion group emails. The Recovery Group, OA12StepsforCOES, Food Addicts Anonymous, OA Primary Purpose, Recovery from Food Addiction (RFA) and The Body Knows email discussion groups are not affiliated with Overeaters Anonymous Inc.

Are there free meditations here?
- No

The Recovery Group
http://www.therecoverygroup.org/

Are there online email discussion groups?
- Yes

How do I get a list of online email discussion groups?
- Online OA & 12 Step Recovery email discussion groups are hosted by •
  OA12StepforCOES • The Recovery Group • OA Primary Purpose • Recovery
  from Food Addiction (RFA) • The Body Knows. People go to the Discussion
  Group's website address and join the discussion group by using their individual
  email to post and receive messages. Individuals will receive emails from the
  discussion group at the individual's email address. People may post, discuss,
  and talk to other members in response to topics and discussion.
  The Recovery Group, OA12StepsforCOES, OA Primary Purpose,
  Recovery from Food Addiction (RFA) and The Body Knows email discussion
  groups are not affiliated with Overeaters Anonymous Inc.
- Go to: http://www.therecoverygroup.org/map/sitemap.html.
  Click on and join the email discussion groups you want to join.
- The Recovery Group Online Discussion Groups
  The main focus of all TRG support groups is twelve step recovery from
  compulsive eating. In addition, certain loops will have a secondary focus, as
  noted below.

AGE
- Kids - http://www.therecoverygroup.org/discovery/kids/index.html
- Teens - http://www.therecoverygroup.org/special/teens.html
- Silver (over 50) - http://www.therecoverygroup.org/special/silver.html

CROSS-ADDICTION
- AA - http://www.therecoverygroup.org/odat/aa/index.html
- Anger - http://www.therecoverygroup.org/odat/anger.html
- Drug Abuse - http://www.therecoverygroup.org/special/dabuse.html
- Love and Sex - http://www.therecoverygroup.org/odat/slaa/
- Spending - http://www.therecoverygroup.org/odat/spending/index.html

FAITH
- Christian - http://www.therecoverygroup.org/odat/christian/index.html
- Jewish - http://www.therecoverygroup.org/odat/jewish/index.html
- Latterday Saints - http://www.therecoverygroup.org/odat/
  latterdaysaints/index.html
- Pagan - http://www.therecoverygroup.org/odat/pagan/index.html

FAMILY & FRIENDS

- **Abuse** - http://www.therecoverygroup.org/odat/abuse/index.html
- **CoKids** - http://www.therecoverygroup.org/cokids/index.html
- **Divorce** - http://www.therecoverygroup.org/odat/divorce/index.html
- **FFOA** - http://www.therecoverygroup.org/odat/pms/index.html
- **Grief** - http://www.therecoverygroup.org/special/grief.html
- **Isolation** - http://www.therecoverygroup.org/odat/isolation/index.html
- **OA Anon** - http://www.therecoverygroup.org/special/oaanon.html
- **Parenting** - http://www.therecoverygroup.org/odat/parenting/index.html
- **Rainbow To Abstinence** - http://www.therecoverygroup.org/odat/rainbow/index.html
- **Relationships** - http://www.therecoverygroup.org/special/relationships.html

FOOD BASED

- **Abstinence** - http://www.therecoverygroup.org/odat/abstinence/index.html
- **The Abstinent Kitchen** - http://www.therecoverygroup.org/discovery/kitchen/index.html

HEALTH

- **Anorexia/Bulimia** - http://www.therecoverygroup.org/special/anorexbul.html
- **Cancer** - http://www.therecoverygroup.org/odat/cancer/index.html
- **Depression** - http://www.therecoverygroup.org/odat/depression/index.html
- **Diabetes** - http://www.therecoverygroup.org/special/diabetes.html
- **Disabilities** - http://www.therecoverygroup.org/odat/disabilities/index.html
- **Emotions** - http://www.therecoverygroup.org/special/emotions.html
- **Homebound** - http://www.therecoverygroup.org/odat/homebound/index.html
- **Isolation** - http://www.therecoverygroup.org/odat/isolation/index.html
- **Pain** - http://www.therecoverygroup.org/odat/pain/index.html
- **PMS** - http://www.therecoverygroup.org/odat/pms/index.html
- **Pregnancy & Motherhood** - http://www.therecoverygroup.org/odat/pregnancy/index.html
- **Weight Loss Surgery** - http://www.therecoverygroup.org/odat/wls/index.html

INTERNATIONAL
- **Deutchland OA** - http://www.therecoverygroup.org/special/german.html
- **Espana OA** - http://www.therecoverygroup.org/special/spanish.html
- **France OA** - http://www.therecoverygroup.org/special/french.html
- **Israel** - http://www.therecoverygroup.org/special/israel.html
- **Italia OA** - http://www.therecoverygroup.org/special/italian.html

PROGRAM RELATED
- **90 In 90** - http://www.therecoverygroup.org/90meetings/index.html
- **Abstinence** - http://www.therecoverygroup.org/odat/abstinence/index.html
- **Grey Sheet** - http://www.therecoverygroup.org/odat/greysheet/index.html
- **HOW** - http://www.therecoverygroup.org/odat/how/index.html
- **Journey to Recovery** - http://www.therecoverygroup.org/jtr/index.html
- **Meditations & Recovery** - http://www.therecoverygroup.org/meditations/index.html
- **OAFriends** - http://www.therecoverygroup.org/oafriends/index.html
- **OA Newcomers** - http://www.therecoverygroup.org/special/newcomers.html
- **OARecovery** - http://www.therecoverygroup.org/recovery/index.html
- **OAsis** - http://www.therecoverygroup.org/oasis.html
- **Relapse** - http://www.therecoverygroup.org/special/relapse.html
- **Sponsor/Sponsee Talk** - http://www.therecoverygroup.org/sponsorsponseetalk.html
- **Strong Recovery** - http://www.therecoverygroup.org/odat/strongrecovery/index.html
- **The Big Book** - http://www.therecoverygroup.org/special/bbrecovery.html
- **WTS** - http://www.therecoverygroup.org/wts/index.html

SPECIAL INTEREST
- **Creative** - http://www.therecoverygroup.org/odat/creative/index.html
- **Exercise** - http://www.therecoverygroup.org/discovery/exercise/index.html
- **The Yellow Brick Road** - http://www.therecoverygroup.org/discovery/yellowbrickroad/index.html

WEIGHT RELATED
- **200 Plus** - http://www.therecoverygroup.org/hotj/200plus.html
- **Hot J** - http://www.therecoverygroup.org/hotj/index.html
- **Weight Loss Surgery** - http://www.therecoverygroup.org/odat/wls/index.html

Are there free meditations here?

- Yes

How do I get free email meditations?

- Send an email to:
  recoverymeditations-subscribe-request@lists.therecoverygroup.org
  to receive email meditations.
  Send an email to:
  meditations-subscribe-request@lists.therecoverygroup.org
  to join an email discussion group to discuss the meditation of the day.
- Free email meditations are often available from Online Discussion Groups.
  You may join Online Discussion Groups hosted by other groups to receive free
  email meditations.

Email
Resources

Greysheeters Anonymous (GSA)

http://www.greysheet.org/cms/
GSA World Services or GSAWS, Inc.
Cherokee Station
PO Box 20098
New York, NY 10021-0061
uscontacts@greysheet.org
phonelist@greysheet.org

Are there online email discussion groups?
- Yes

How do I get a list of online email discussion groups?
- Subscribe to the monthly list publication at:
  http://www.greysheet.org/cms/international-contacts.html, which lists hundreds of members worldwide, including available sponsors.
- Join GreyNet - Post a request to this online group, to obtain a sponsor's phone number privately.
- To subscribe to the greynet, send a blank email to:
  greynet-subscribe@yahoogroups.com.
- Join Online Greysheeters Anonymous Forums:
  To visit and join Greysheet Forums go to:
  http://www.greysheet.org/forum/.
  Group's website address from their Internet and join the discussion group by using their individual email to post and receive messages. Individuals will receive emails from the discussion group at the individual's email address. People may post, discuss, and talk to other members in response to topics and discussion in the discussion group through email responses to discussion group emails. The Recovery Group, OA12StepsforCOES, OA Primary Purpose, Recovery from Food Addiction (RFA), Greynet, and The Body Knows email discussion groups are not affiliated with Overeaters Anonymous Inc.

Are there free meditations here?
- No

Food Addiction: The Body Knows
http://www.kaysheppard.com/
kshepp825@aol.com
321-727-8040

Are there online email discussion groups?
- **Yes**

How do I get a list of online email discussion groups?
- **To join "The Body Knows" send a blank email to:**
  (thebodyknows-subscribe@yahoogroups.com)
  The discussion group is a group of people who use the plan of eating suggested in the book *Food Addiction: The Body Knows*, 1989 by Kay Sheppard. Started in 2000, "Food Addiction: The Body Knows" is a website (http://www.kaysheppard.com) and online discussion group operated by Kay Sheppard, nutritionist and food counselor.

Anorexics & Bulemics Anonymous
http://www.anorexicsandbulimicsanonymousaba.com/
Main P.O. Box 125 | Edmonton, AB T5J 2G9
780-443-6077

Are there online email discussion groups?
- **No**

Are there free meditations here?
- **No**

12 Steps for Compulsive Overeaters (OA12StepsforCOES)
Online 12 Step Group for Compulsive Overeaters

OA Inc. Registered Intergroup
http://www.oa12step4coes.org
sunlight@oa12step4coes.org

Are there online email discussion groups?
- **Yes**

How do I get a list of online email discussion groups?
- **Go to:** http://www.oa12step4coes.org/loops.html **or the website address
here for each email discussion group. Click on each of the loops and then
enter your email address in the subscription box of the newly opened page**

OA Meeting Email Discussion Loops
- **Loop Meeting 4 Compulsive Overeaters:**
  http://www.oa12step4coes.org/loops/meeting.html

Special Focus OA Sharing Email Discussion Loops
- **Recovery 4 Relapse:**
  http://www.oa12step4coes.org/loops/relapse.html
- **Sponsors 4 Today:**
  http://www.oa12step4coes.org/loops/sponsorloop.html
- **Healing Abuse & Compulsive Overeating:**
  http://www.oa12step4coes.org/loops/abuse.html
- **Chronic Illness or Injury and Compulsive Overeating:**
  http://www.oa12step4coes.org/loops/illness.html
- **Emotional Health Issues and Compulsive Overeating:**
  http://www.oa12step4coes.org/loops/emotional.html
- **12 Step 4 Christian Compulsive Overeaters:**
  http://www.oa12step4coes.org/loops/christian.html
- **Rainbow 12 Step 4 Compulsive Overeaters:**
  http://www.oa12step4coes.org/loops/rainbow.html
- **12 Step 4 Codependent Compulsive Overeaters:**
  http://www.oa12step4coes.org/loops/coda.html

<u>OA Study Email Discussion Loops</u>

- **Big Book 12 Step 4 Compulsive Overeaters:**
  http://www.oa12step4coes.org/loops/bb.html
- **Traditions 12 Step 4 Compulsive Overeaters:**
  http://www.oa12step4coes.org/loops/traditionsloop.html
- **Online OA & 12 Step Recovery email discussion groups are hosted by**
- **OA12StepforCOES • The Recovery Group • OA Primary Purpose • Recovery from Food Addiction (RFA) • The Body Knows. People go to the Discussion Group's website address from their Internet and join the discussion group by using their individual email to post and receive messages. Individuals will receive emails from the discussion group at the individual's email address. People may post, discuss, and talk to other members in response to topics and discussion. The Recovery Group, OA12StepsforCOES, OA Primary Purpose, Recovery from Food Addiction (RFA) and The Body Knows email discussion groups are not affiliated with Overeaters Anonymous Inc.**

Are there free meditations here?
- **No**

Recovery from Food Addiction (RFA)

http://health.groups.yahoo.com/group/recoveryfromfoodaddiction/
recoveryfromfoodaddiction-subscribe@yahoogroups.com
P.O. Box 35543
713-673-2848

Are there online email discussion groups?
- **Yes**

How do I get a list of online email discussion groups?
- **Subscribe to:** recoveryfromfoodaddiction-subscribe@yahoogroups.com
  to join.
  Or Click on:
  http://health.groups.yahoo.com/group/recoveryfromfoodaddiction/
  and Join.
- **Online OA & 12 Step Recovery email discussion groups are hosted by • OA12StepforCOES • The Recovery Group • OA Primary Purpose • Recovery from Food Addiction (RFA) • The Body Knows. People go to the Discussion Group's website address from their Internet and join the discussion group by using their individual email to post and receive messages. Individuals will receive emails from the discussion group at the individual's email address. People may post, discuss, and talk to other members in response to topics and discussion in the dicscussion group through email responses to discussion group emails. The Recovery Group, OA12StepsforCOES, OA Primary Purpose, Recovery from Food Addiction (RFA) and The Body Knows email discussion groups are not affiliated with Overeaters Anonymous Inc**

Are there free meditations here?
- **No**

OA Primary Purpose

http://www.oapp.info/oaprimarypurposegroups
http://health.groups.yahoo.com/group/oapp/links
oapp-subscribe@yahoogroups.com
712-432-3900 PIN 643578#

Are there online email discussion groups?
- Yes

How do I get a list of online email discussion groups?
- The yahoogroups discussion group is used in conjunstion with the SKYPE OAPP phone meeting. The discussion group is used for people to receive questions and answers that will be read at the SKYPE phone meeting.
- To get started send an email to the Host of the Skype Open Big Book Study Meetings to Request an Invitation: OAPP Coordinator: Joni P. at joni@oapp.info.
- You will receive an email back confirming you have been added to the Yahoogroups discussion group to receive the list of questions and answers each day.
- OAPP Skype Phone Meetings are held on the following days and times:

Day	USA/CST	Speaker	Host	Program	Host
Monday	11:00 AM	Cliff Bishop	Joni B	OA	joni@oapp.info

Are there free meditations here?
- No

The Coffee Shop

712-432-3900 Access PIN: 897578#
Daily - 7 A.M. EST
Recorded meeting:
712-432-3903 Access PIN: 897578#
Press O# for most recent recording
Code for previous recording

Are there online email discussion groups?
- No

The Parking Lot
712-432-3900
Access PIN: 6508933#
Daily - 1 A.M. - 6:30 A.M. EST

Are there online email discussion groups?
- **No**

Are there free meditations here?
- **No**

Cups & Scales
http://groups.yahoo.com/group/cupsscalesgroup
cupsscalesgroup-subscribe@yahoogroups.com

Are there online email discussion groups?
- **Yes**

How do I get a list of online email discussion groups?
- **Send a blank email to:**
  cupsscalesgroup-subscribe@yahoogroups.com, **Or Click on:**
  http://groups.yahoo.com/group/cupsscalesgroup **to Join.**
- **"Cups & Scales is an online discussion group**
  (cupsscalesgroup-subscribe@yahoogroups.com), **started in 2010,**
  to discuss attitudes around life and food trickery. Distorted eating often
  begins with distorted thinking.
- **'Cups & Scales' takes its name from the book** *Cups & Scales, Weighing &*
  Measuring Food & Emotions **by Anonymous Twelve Step Recovery Members.**
  This book is after the famous AA-book *Stools & Bottles* **that discusses**
  character defects of the alcoholic. *Cups & Scales - Weighing & Measuring Food*
  & Emotions - Information & Picture Book is a serious picture Book with humor
  on character defects related to life and food trickery. It is **recommended**
  literature. *Cups & Scales Cookbook - Everything Weighed & Measured -*
  Recipes - No Sugar, Wheat, Flour & Sample Plans of Eating **is** recommended
  literature.
- **'We are not a glum lot' it says in the AA Big Book. With our food trickery and**
  curious twists of mind, we aim to become aware of how the body and mind
  are involved. When the food is "talking ", share to become aware of thoughts
  and attitudes. - fighting, defiance, rebellion, self-pity, and faulty glasses. The
  group takes no position on weighing and measuring food
  (http://groups.yahoo.com/group/cupsscalesgroup).

Overeaters Anonymous Inc. (OA)

http://www.oa.org
PO Box 44020
Rio Rancho, New Mexico 87174-4020 USA
http://www.oa.org/contact.php
505-891-2664

Is there free downloadable literature?
- Yes

Where do I get free downloadable literature?
- The following PDF files appear on various pages within the Web site. They are collected for easy reference and downloading: .
  http://www.oa.org/docs.php
  A Step Ahead Newsletter
  A Step Ahead: Second Quarter 2010 (color)
  A Step Ahead: Second Quarter 2010 (black and white)
  A Step Ahead: First Quarter 2010 (color)
  A Step Ahead: First Quarter 2010 (black and white)
  A Step Ahead: Fourth Quarter 2009 (color)
  A Step Ahead: Fourth Quarter 2009 (black and white)
  A Step Ahead: Third Quarter 2009 (color)
  A Step Ahead: Third Quarter 2009 (black and white)
  Ask-It Basket and Archive
  Ask-It Basket Archive
  Ask-It Basket Questions
  Conference Cassettes or CDs
  Contribute
  Contribution Form
  Seventh Tradition of OA
  Seventh Tradition of OA (Translatable Version)
  Copyright Requests
  Permission to Use the OA Logo
  Reprint Permission Form
  Courier Newsletter
  2010 Courier Newsletter (color)
  2010 Courier Newsletter (black and white)
  2009 Courier newsletter
  Discontinued Literature
  OA Cares flyer

OA Is Not a Diet Club Pamphlet
<u>Family and Friends</u>
Compulsive Overeating: An Inside View
To the Family
Find a Face-to-Face Meeting
OA Intergroup Directory
Group Secretary Materials
Contributions Form
Literature Catalog
Literature Order Form
Registration/Change Form
Secretaries Maintain the Connection
Seventh Tradition of OA
Seventh-Tradition Skits
Strong Meeting Checklist
<u>Group Support</u>
Border Guards: Tradition Four Issues
The Balanced Application of Tradition Four
Designated Downloader Flyer
Excerpt from the OA Handbook
Group Inventory
Guidelines for a Group Conscience Meeting/
Suggested Group Conscience Meeting
Format
How to Start a Meeting
Let People Know About Your Meeting
Lifeline Meeting Format
OA Intergroup Directory
Seventh Tradition of OA
Seventh Tradition of OA (Translatable Version)
Seventh-Tradition Skits
Suggested Meeting Format
Suggested Step-Study Meeting Format
<u>Lifeline</u>
Sample Issue
2009 Lifeline Index
Lifeline Tabletop Display
Lifeline Through the Years
Subscription Forms

Literature

Literature Catalog

Order Form

Materials from WSO's Mailing to Intergroups

First OA Census Yields Great Results

Media/Professionals

Membership Survey Report

Meetings

OA Intergroup Directory

OA Guidelines

Budget Guidelines for Service Bodies

Consensus Guidelines and Board Article

Fundraising and Prudent Reserve Guidelines for Groups and Intergroups

Group Conscience Guidelines/Suggested Group Conscience Meeting Format

Guidelines for Addressing Disruptive Behavior

Guidelines for Health Fair Participation

Guidelines for Locally Produced Literature

Guidelines for Membership Retention

Guidelines for Local Newsletters

Guidelines for OA Events

Guidelines for Public Information Events

Guidelines for Writing the History of Your Local Area

Guidelines for Professional Outreach Committees

Intergroup Treasurer Guidelines

OA Approved Literature List

OA CARES Inmate Correspondence Program Guidelines

Web Site Development Guidelines

OA Literature Translations

Translation Guidelines for OA Literature

Translation Fund Application

OA Regions

Map and Description of the 10 OA Regions

Public Information Suggestions

Billy's Story

Courier Newsletter

Instructions for Getting OA's PSA Aired

Let People Know About Your Meeting

The Twelve Steps and Twelve Traditions of Overeaters Anonymous:

A Kid's View

PI Poster Kit

15 Questions

How to Contact OA
Is Food a Problem for You?
Many Symptoms, One Solution
OA Preamble
Welcome to OA
<u>*Register/Change Face-to-Face Meeting*</u>
Group Registration/Change Form
<u>*Register/Change Online or Telephone Meeting*</u>
Telephone Group Registration/Change Form
Register/Change Service Body
Intergroup Registration/Change Form
National or Language Service Board Registration/Change Form
Virtual Service Board Registration/Change Form
<u>*Service Body Support*</u>
Conference Policy Manual
Delegate Support Fund Application
Delegate Support Fund Contributions
Designated Downloader Flyer
Matching Grant Program Application
Reduced-Cost Literature Application Form
Sample Intergroup Bylaws
Sample Statement of Purpose
OA Bylaws Subpart A
OA Bylaws Subpart B
Seventh Tradition of OA
Seventh Tradition of OA (Translatable Version)
Seventh-Tradition Skits
Service By Mail/Email
Service By Mail/Email Form
Spiritual Principles of the OA Program
Spiritual Principles of the OA Program
Twelfth Step Within
Been Slipping and Sliding? A Reading and Writing Tool
Planning a Sponsorship Workshop
Recovery Insurance Policy
Twelfth Step Within Speakers Sign Up Form
<u>Youth in OA</u>

Billy's Story pamphlet

Suggested Meeting Format for Young People
The Twelve Steps and Twelve Traditions: A Kid's View booklet

How do I get free recordings for download?

- Go to http://www.oa.org; Click on PODCASTS" in the upper lefthand corner of the webpage; Go to http://www.oa.org/podcast. Free Recordings/ PODCASTS available in iTunes & MP3.

Overeaters Anonymous Podcast- #18: Interview with Charles: March 18, 2010 at 3:02 pm: In this edition, OA member Charles talks about his relationship with food and his recovery from compulsive eating in Overeaters Anonymous.

Overeaters Anonymous Podcast- #17: "OA Members Come in All Sizes: Welcome, Whatever Your Problem with Food."
January 13, 2010 at 3:57 pm: In this edition, we have a partial reading of the pamphlet "OA Members Come in All Sizes: Welcome, Whatever Your Problem with Food

Overeaters Anonymous Podcast- #16: "To the Man Who Wants to Stop Compulsive Overeating, Welcome." December 9, 2009 at 8:39 pm: In this edition, we have a reading of the pamphlet "To the Man Who Wants to Stop Compulsive Overeating, Welcome"

Overeaters Anonymous Podcast- #15: "Welcome Home": October 30, 2009 at 5:38 pm: In this edition, we have a reading of a member-written story called "Welcome Home" from the OA book Lifeline Sampler.

Overeaters Anonymous Podcast- #14: Interview with Maria: August 19, 2009 at 8:50 am: This podcast is in Spanish.

Overeaters Anonymous Podcast- #13: Interview with Carolina: August 19, 2009 at 8:49 am: This podcast is in Spanish.

Overeaters Anonymous Podcast- #12: Interview with Ana: August 19, 2009 at 8:42 am: This podcast is in Spanish.

Overeaters Anonymous Podcast- #11: Interview with Esti: June 5, 2009 at 9:50 pm: Welcome to the Overeaters Anonymous (OA) Podcast. In this edition, OA member Esti talks about her involvement and Overeaters Anonymous.

Overeaters Anonymous Podcast- #10: Interview with Joe: April 20, 2009 at 8:46 pm: In this edition, OA member Joe talks about his relationship with food and Overeaters Anonymous.

Overeaters Anonymous Podcast- #9: Interview with Dodie: February 2, 2009 at 6:43 pm: In this edition, OA member Dodie talks about her relationship with food and the circumstances that brought her to OA.

Overeaters Anonymous Podcast- #8: Interview with Bob: January 5, 2009 at 4:26 pm: In this edition, OA member Bob discusses the circumstances that brought him to OA and his experiences.

Overeaters Anonymous Podcast- #7: Interview with Kathleen: November 14, 2008 at 6:54 pm: In this edition, OA member Kathleen discusses the circumstances that brought her to OA and her experiences.

Overeaters Anonymous Podcast- #6: OA meeting: October 6, 2008 at 4:52 pm: In this edition, We recap a Friday Morning OA meeting.

Overeaters Anonymous Podcast- #5: Interview with Beth: September 3, 2008 at 9:54 pm: In this edition, OA member Beth discusses the circumstances that brought her to OA and her experiences.

Overeaters Anonymous Podcast- #4: Interview with Bob: July 10, 2008 at 3:06 pm: In this edition, OA member Bob discusses the circumstances that brought him to OA and how his involvement with OA has improved his life.

Overeaters Anonymous Podcast- #3: Interview with Mary: June 9, 2008 at 8:11 pm: In this edition, OA member Mary discusses what motivated her to seek out OA and how her involvement with OA has helped her.

Overeaters Anonymous Podcast- #2: Interview with AJ: May 10, 2008 at 6:13 pm: In this edition, OA member AJ discusses her relationship with food, what brought her to OA and how her involvement with OA has helped her in the recovery process.

Overeaters Anonymous Podcast- #1: Introduction: April 10, 2008 at 6:11 pm: This is the first Overeaters Anonymous (OA) Podcast. In this edition, Managing Director, Naomi L. and OA member and Chairman, Dodie H. discuss what OA is and how it can help.

How do I get the free recording downloads from OA Regions 1-10?

- There are many MP3 recordings & PODCASTS at the OA Region 1-10 websites here:
- **OA Region 1 Media Library:** http://oaregion1.org/Tape/Media%20Library%20CD's%20for%20USA.pdf
  There are over 74 tapes/CDs in the Region 1 Tape Library to benefit all. There is no cost to you, except postage to return the tapes when you're done. Please save and re-use the shipping envelope. A mailing label for return is sent with each order.
- **OA Region 2 Media Library:** http://www.oar2.org/index.php?option=com_content&view=article&id=176&Itemid=49
  Live Feed To Subscribe To: http://www.oar2.org/index.php?option=com_podcast&view=feed&format=raw&Itemid=100
  Speakers & PODCASTS are available for Download and Live Listening.
- **OA Region 3: No Media Library**
- **OA Region 4: No Media Library**

- **OA Region 5 Media Library:** http://region5oa.org/wordpress/
  Region 5 Convention Sessions are available for MP# listening.
- **OA Region 6: No Media Library**
- **OA Region 7 Media Library:** http://oaregion7.org/resources/
  OA Region 7 Speakers From the Assembly may be heard in MP3 recordings.
- **OA Region 8: No Media Library**
- **OA Region 9: No Media Library**
- **OA Region 10: No Media Library**

What is approved literature?

http://bookstore.oa.org/quickform.php

- **AA Approved Literature**
- **OA Approved Literature**
- ***Pamphlets, Booklets and Wallet Cards***

Group Registration Forms

Extra catalogs Free

Extra order forms Free

Membership Survey Report

Recovery Checklist

Many Symptoms, One Solution

Person to Person

Think First wallet card

OA Members Come in All Sizes

OA Handbook for Members, Groups & Intergroups

A Program of Recovery

Dignity of Choice

A Commitment to Abstinence

A Plan of Eating: A Tool for Living-One Day at a Time

Before You Take That First Compulsive Bite, Remember ...

The Tools of Recovery

Questions and Answers

If God Spoke to OA

Welcome Back

What If I Don't Believe in "God"?

Sponsorship Kit

A Guide for Sponsors

A Guide to the Twelve Steps for You and Your Sponsor

The Twelve Traditions of OA

To the Family of the Compulsive Overeater

To Parents and Concerned Adults

To the Newcomer
To the Teen
Black OA Members Share Their Experience,Strength and Hope
To the Man Who Wants to Stop Compulsive
Overeating, Welcome
Maintaining a Healthy Weight
Compulsive Overeating: An Inside View
The Twelve Concepts of OA Service
Anonymity
Members in Relapse
Just for Today wallet card
One Day at a Time wallet card
Pocket Reference for OA Members

I Put My Hand in Yours

Bulletin Board Attraction Card
New-Prospect Card
Twelfth-Step-Within Handbook
I Put My Hand in Yours (Red Book)
Fourth-Step Inventory Guide
Suggested Meeting Format
Recovery from Relapse Meeting Format
Young People's Meeting Format
Lifeline Meeting Format
Suggested Step-Study Meeting Format
OA Guidelines
Sample Intergroup Bylaws
Intergroup Starter Kit
Newcomer Packet
Recovery from Relapse Packet
Focus on Anorexia and Bulimia Packet
New Group Starter Kit
Newcomer Meeting Leader's Kit
Young People's Meeting Kit
Is Food a Problem for You?
About OA
The Courier: a Newsletter for the
Professional Community (2010 ed.)
Introducing OA to Health Care Professionals
Fifteen Questions
To the Teen Questionnaire

Hearing Is Believing:
OA Members Speak ... (CD)
OA Recovery Brochures (CD)
The Twelve Steps and Twelve Traditions
of OA (CD)
Recovery Coins
Serenity Prayer Coin
Recovery Medallion
Anniversary Medallions.
30-day Recovery Coin
60-day Recovery Coin
90-day Recovery Coin
6-month Recovery Coin
9-month Recovery Coin
Newcomer Welcome Coin

Where can I buy the approved literature?

- http://bookstore.oa.org/quickform.php;
- http://www.oa.org
- http://www.aa.org
- http://www.amazon.com **and other bookstores**

CEA-HOW (Compulsive Overeaters Anonymous-HOW)

> http://www.ceahow.org/
> 5500 E. Atherton St., Suite 227-B
> Long Beach, CA 90815-4017
> 562-342-9344
> CEA-HOW General Service Office: gso@ceahow

Is there free downloadable literature?

- Yes

Where do I get free downloadable literature?

- **The following PDF files appear on various pages within this Web site. They are collected for easy reference and downloading.**

- **The How Concept:** http://www.ceahow.org/ceahow/sites/default/files/readings/CEA-HOWConcept.pdf
- **The Twelve Steps:** http://www.ceahow.org/ceahow/sites/default/files/readings/12Steps.pdf
- **The Twelve Traditions:** http://www.ceahow.org/ceahow/sites/default/files/readings/12Traditions.pdf
- **7 Tools:** http://www.ceahow.org/ceahow/sites/default/files/readings/7Tools.pdf
- **AA Big Book - Step Prayers:** http://www.ceahow.org/ceahow/sites/default/files/readings/Prayers.pdf
- **Just for Today:** http://www.ceahow.org/ceahow/sites/default/files/readings/Just4Today.pdf
- **Steps 10, 11, 12:** http://tinyurl.com/2vt9mro
- **Steps 8 & 9:** http://tinyurl.com/369uuke
- **Steps 6 & 7:** http://tinyurl.com/37nbpqh
- **Steps 4 & 5:** http://tinyurl.com/37nbpqh
- **Steps 1, 2 & 3:** http://tinyurl.com/36vrwwd
- **Absinent Holidays:** http://tinyurl.com/32b73sq
- **The 7 Tools:** http://tinyurl.com/344tl8b
- **The Sponsorship Chairperson:** http://tinyurl.com/395tru9
- **Back to Basics:** http://tinyurl.com/3y6sb6p
- **Sponsorship Workshop Format:** http://tinyurl.com/3a9jprj
- **Food Letter:** http://tinyurl.com/36mfxq8

How do I get free recordings for download?

- **Using Slips Wisely - Sunday October 18, 2009 download/play mp3:**
  http://www.ceahow.org/mp3s/lois_using_slips_wisely.mp3
- **2 for 1 Sponsorship - Sunday January 31, 2010 - download/play wav format:**
  http://www.ceahow.org/mp3s/2-1Sponsorship-1-31-2010.wav
- **Sponsoring Chronic Relapsers - Sunday March 14, 2010 - download/play mp3:**
  http://www.ceahow.org/mp3s/March14-2010-sponsor-chronic-relapsers.mp3
- **Traveling in Abstinence and Medical Abstinence, Sunday April 18. Replay is available at: 712-432-1284 Code: 152077# download/play mp3:**
  http://www.ceahow.org/mp3s/April18-2010TravelMedicalAbstinence.mp3

What is approved literature?

- <u>Pamphlets</u>
  Abstinence Model
  Welcome Newcomer
  A View of Medical Abstinence
  Am I A Food Addict?
  If God Spoke to CEA-HOW
  Overview of the 12 Steps
  The CEA-HOW Concept
  The Meaning of Abstinence
  Weighing & Measuring
  What is Food Addiction?
  Just for Today (Card)
  One Day At A Time (Card)
  Affirmations (Card)
  Achieving Balance Cookbook
  Meeting Support Structures
  Healthcare Letter
  Meeting Financial Record
  Sign-in Sheets
  2nd Group Starter Kit
  Working the Program
  Just Desserts Questions
  Steps 6 thru 12 Questions
  After the Inventory Questions
  Recommitment Questions
  Kaleidoscope

Maintenance Guide Book
Workbook, AA Big Book
Came to Believe Questions
Pioneer Questions
As Bill Sees It Questions
Twelve Traditions Study Guide
<u>Articles:</u>
Steps 10, 11, 12
Steps 8 & 9
Steps 6 & 7
Steps 4 & 5
Steps 1, 2 & 3
Absinent Holidays
The 7 Tools
The Sponsorship Chairperson
Back to Basics
Sponsorship Workshop Format
Food Letter

Where can I buy the approved literature?

- **Click on:** http://www.ceahow.org/?q=node/9 **to purchase from CEAHOW Store**

Food Addicts Anonymous, Inc.

http://www.foodaddictsanonymous.org/meetings-events
561-967-3871

Is there free downloadable literature?

- Yes

Where do I get free downloadable literature?

- Click on http://www.foodaddictsanonymous.org/catalog/13

What is approved literature?

- FAA Food Plan
  There is an FAA plan of eating. The FAA plan of eating is found on the
  website: http://www.foodaddictsanonymous.org/faa-food-plan.
  It includes fruit, dairy, protein, and vegetables, grains and starches. People

- **Pamphlets & Books**
  Newcomer's Packet
  Newcomer's Packet (Special Packet of 10)
  Newcomer's Book Bundle
  Abstinent Cooking for Food Addicts
  Annual Menu Planner and Journal
  Food Addicts Anonymous
  FAA Steps to Recovery
  Food For the Soul
  A Guide to Abstinence
  Information Pamphlet
  Names of Sugar, Flour and Wheat
  A Path to Freedom
  Sponsorship Pamphlet
  Understanding Food Addiction and Why Abstinence is Necessary
  The Abstinent Times 1 Year
  The Abstinent Times 2 Years
  The Abstinent Times Back Issues
  FAA Seventh Step Prayer Card
  FAA Chips-Welcome (white), 30, 60, 90 days
  FAA Medallions-1 mo, 6 mo, 1yr to 21 yrs
  Food Diary
  Just For Today
  Wallet Menu Card

Where can I buy the approved literature?

- **Click on:**
  http://www.foodaddictsanonymous.org/catalog/13
  http://www.foodaddictsanonymous.org/catalog/6
  http://www.foodaddictsanonymous.org
  http://bookstore.oa.org/quickform.php;
  http://www.aa.org
  http://www.amazon.com **and other bookstores**

The Recovery Group

http://www.therecoverygroup.org/

Are there free meditations here?
- Yes

How do I get free email meditations?
- **Send an email to:**
  recoverymeditations-subscribe-request@lists.therecoverygroup.org
  to receive email meditations.
  Send an email to:
  meditations-subscribe-request@lists.therecoverygroup.org
  to join an email discussion group to discuss the meditation of the day.
- **Free email meditations are often available from Online Discussion Groups. You may join Online Discussion Groups hosted by other groups to receive free email meditations.**

Is there free downloadable literature?
- Yes

Where do I get free downloadable literature?
- **The following PDF files appear on various pages within the Web site. They are collected for easy reference and downloading: .**
- **30 Questions:** http://www.therecoverygroup.org/questions/index.html
- **Ten Ways To Love Ourselves:** http://www.therecoverygroup.org/jtr/love_ourselves.html
- **Cancer:** http://www.therecoverygroup.org/cancer/index.html
- **Danny's Letters to God:** http://www.therecoverygroup.org/danny/dannytogod.html
- **Inspirations:** http://www.therecoverygroup.org/inspirations/index.html
- **Odyssey:** http://www.therecoverygroup.org/odyssey/index.html
- **Recovery Meditations:** http://www.therecoverygroup.org/meditations/index.html
- **Reflections of Recovery:** http://www.therecoverygroup.org/jtr/journals.html
- **Reflections of the Twelve Steps:** http://www.therecoverygroup.org/jtr/12steps.html

- **The Promises:** http://www.therecoverygroup.org/support/promise1.html
- **The Serenity Prayer:** http://www.therecoverygroup.org/jtr/serenity.html
- **Speakers:** http://www.therecoverygroup.org/speakers/index.html
- *Serendipity ~ The Recovery Newsletter*: http://www.therecoverygroup.org/serendipity/index.html

---

What is approved literature?
- **Not Specified**

Where can I buy recovery literature?
- http://bookstore.oa.org/quickform.php;
- http://www.oa.org
- http://www.aa.org
- http://www.amazon.com **and other bookstores**

Greysheeters Anonymous (GSA)

http://www.greysheet.org/cms/
GSA World Services or GSAWS, Inc.
Cherokee Station
PO Box 20098
New York, NY 10021-0061
uscontacts@greysheet.org
phonelist@greysheet.org

Are there free meditations here?
- **No**

How do I get free meditations?
- Free email meditations are often available from other Online Discussion Groups. You may join Online Discussion Groups hosted by other groups to receive free email meditations.

Where do I get free downloadable literature?
- The following PDF files appear on various pages within the Web site. They are collected for easy reference and downloading:
  Go to: http://www.greysheet.org/cms/literature.html
  GSA Preamble
  Group Purpose
  12 Steps
  12 Traditions
  12 Promises
  Pamphlets
  Shades of Grey Archives

How do I get free recordings for download?
- Audio Qualifications: Taped when the qualifier led a live meeting.
  Go go: http://www.greysheet.org/cms/member-resources.html to download free literature & audio.
  Cruises: A section devoted to the unique situation of weighing and measuring at sea.
  Holidays: Greysheeters Anonymous members' sharing their Experience, Strength, and Hope about getting through holidays and celebrations abstinently.

No Matter What: A collection of stories from fourteen writers who were part of a writing group, chronicling times when they stayed abstinent under a myriad of circumstances.

Our Disease, Our Solution: Greysheeters Anonymous members' descriptions of the three fold nature of compulsive eating and how the GreySheet program addresses each.

What Kept Me Abstinent: Members sharing what tools they use to stay abstinent without exception.

Written Qualifications: Stories shared by GreySheet members who have attained at least 90 days of back to back GreySheet abstinence, telling "what it was like, what happened, and what it is like now."

What is approved literature?

- **AA Approved Literature**
- *Shades of Grey Newsletters*
- *Shades of Grey Book*
- *GreySheet Stories Book*
- *GreySheet Wallet Cards*
- *Pamphlet - "A Solution for Compulsive Eaters"*

Where can I buy the approved literature?

- **Go to:** http://www.greysheet.org/cms/literature.html to purchase literature.
- **Send an email request to:** gsaliterature@greysheet.org

What is other literature referring to the Greysheet Food Plan?

- *Greysheet Recipes Collection: Recipes from Members of Greysheet Recipes Yahoo Forum:* Greysheet Abstinent Recipes with Weighed & Measured Amounts in Recipe Servings

Where can I buy literature referring to the Greysheet Food Plan?

- **Go to:** http://www.greysheetrecipes.org
- **Go to:** http://www.amazon.com

Food Addiction: The Body Knows

http://www.kaysheppard.com/
kshepp825@aol.com
321-727-8040

Is there free downloadable literature?

- Yes

Where do I get free downloadable literature?

- **The following PDF files appear on various pages within the Web site.**
  http://www.kaysheppard.com/articles.htm
- **<u>Articles</u>**
  What is Food Addiction?
  The Biochemistry of Food Addiction
  Body Awareness
  Making Appropriate Choices
  Dealing With Denial
  Revised Food Plan
  "First Bite" Concept
  Recovery During the Holidays
  Each Day -- A New Beginning
  Getting Physically Clean
  Powerless and Unmanageable
  Avoiding Food Addiction Relapse
  Dealing With Stress in Recovery - Part I
  Dealing With Stress in Recovery - Part II
  Why a Weighed and Measured Food Plan?
  10th Step Inventory Checklist for Food Addicts
  Surviving the Flu in Recovery
  Holiday Compulsive Shopping and Spendin g
  Food Addicts' Drunk and Impaired Driving
  Stephanie Z.'s Story and the significance of Step 10 for long-term Recovery

What is approved literature?

- *Food Addiction: The Body Knows*, 1989, by Kay Sheppard.
- *From the First Bite*, 1989, by Kay Sheppard

Where can I buy the approved literature?

- http://www.kaysheppard.com
- http://www.amazon.com **and other bookstores**

Anorexics & Bulimics Anonymous

http://www.anorexicsandbulimicsanonymousaba.com/
Main P.O. Box 125 | Edmonton, AB T5J 2G9
780-443-6077

Are there free meditations here?
- No

Is there free downloadable literature?
- No

What is approved literature?
- <u>Book</u>
  Anorexics & Bulemics Anonymous Book (288 pages)
- <u>Pamphlets</u>
  Anorexics and Bulimics Anonymous – A 12-Step Fellowship and recovery program for women and men with eating disorders.
  Anorexics and Bulimics Anonymous for the Compulsive Eater
  Mini Book
  Speaker CD Sets
  The Family Perspective 3 CD set
  The Promises 4 CD set
  The Steps 6 CD set
  The Tools 6 CD set
  The Traditions 5 CD set
  What It's Like Now: A Message of Hope' 5 CD set
  1st International Conference 9 CD set

Where can I buy the approved literature?
- **Send an email to:** aba@shawbiz.ca **to order.**
  http://www.anorexicsandbulimicsanonymousaba.com/

Literature

12 Steps for Compulsive Overeaters (OA12StepsforCOES)
Online 12 Step Group for Compulsive Overeaters

OA Inc. Registered Intergroup
http://www.oa12step4coes.org
sunlight@oa12step4coes.org

Are there free meditations here?
- No

Is there free downloadable literature?
- Yes

Where do I get free downloadable literature?
- Go to: http://www.oa12step4coes.org/resources.html
  or to the website addresses here.
- *The Big Book - Alcoholics Anonymous:*
  http://www.aa.org/bigbookonline/en_tableofcnt.cfm
- *The OA Lifeline:*
  http://www.oa.org/lifeline-magazine/
- *The AA Grapevine:*
  http://www.aagrapevine.org/gv/current/
- *In the Sunlight (Newsletter):*
  http://www.oa12step4coes.org/news/sunlight.html
  Go to the listings under OA Inc.
  www.oa.org *for free downloadable literature*

How do I get free recordings for download?
- There are many MP3 recordings at the OA Regions 1-10 websites. Go to the
  listings under OA Inc. for OA Regions.

What is approved literature?
- AA Approved Literature
- OA Approved Literature
- The Twelve Steps and Twelve Traditions of Overeaters Anonymous
- The OA Twelve-Step Workbook
- Alcoholics Anonymous, 4th Edition

Where can I buy the approved literature?

- http://www.oa12step4coes.org/resources.html
- http://bookstore.oa.org/quickform.php;
- http://www.aa.org
- http://www.amazon.com **and other bookstores**

Recovery from Food Addiction (RFA)

http://health.groups.yahoo.com/group/recoveryfromfoodaddiction/
recoveryfromfoodaddiction-subscribe@yahoogroups.com
P.O. Box 35543
713-673-2848

Are there free meditations here?

- **No**

Is there free downloadable literature?

- Yes

Where do I get free downloadable literature?

- *Food Type Grid: Daily Portions*
  Weekly Food Planner Grid: One Weeks Food Planner
- *To get these documents:*
  Join the online discussion group Recovery from Food Addiction
  Send a blank email to:
  recoveryfromfoodaddiction-subscribe@yahoogroups.com
  After you have joined and received your confirmation, go to your yahoogroups:
  http://health.groups.yahoo.com/group/recoveryfromfoodaddiction/)."
  Go to your Group: Recovery from Food Addiction.
  Go to Files in the lefthand column on the homepage.
  You will find a list of face-to-face meetings.

What is approved literature?

- **Food Addiction: The Body Knows**

Where can I buy the approved literature?

- http://www.amazon.com **and other bookstores**

OA Primary Purpose

http://www.oapp.info/oaprimarypurposegroups
http://health.groups.yahoo.com/group/oapp/links
oapp-subscribe@yahoogroups.com
712-432-3900 PIN 643578#

Is there free downloadable literature?
- **Yes**

Where do I get free downloadable literature?
- **Big Book Download download a searchable version (e-aa lite is free)**
  http://anonpress.org/choices/

How do I get downloadable recordings?
- **Audio -- OAPP Weekly BB Study Meetings**
  Tuesdays and Fridays -- Also Includes Mondays with Cliff
  http://www.mediafire.com/
  ?sharekey=a2194263c7a02e959bf8d6369220dcabeb6410a8e70
  daf835be6ba49b5870170
- **Audio -- OAPP Weekly Foundation Meetings   Tuesdays**
  http://www.mediafire.com/
  ?sharekey=a2194263c7a02e959bf8d6369220dcaba3460315d3a15d
  40ce018c8114394287
- **OAPP Audio Recordings**
  http://www.mediafire.com/
  ?sharekey=eeaf9311056cc601ableab3e9fa335cae81c3d8f784e0df0
- **Recording of Cliff Bishop Leading Angel Through the Steps**
  http://www.mediafire.com/file/omkiyomnnyn/12 Stepping with Cliff &
  Angel.mp3
- **Recording of Joni Berman's Story and the Origins of OAPP (Primary Purpose)**
  -- Part 1
  http://www.mediafire.com/?ygm3zyvddmz
- **Recording of Joni Berman's Story and the Origins of OAPP (Primary Purpose)**
  -- Part 2
  http://www.mediafire.com/?jbz2tn2wqkn
- **Recording of Questions and Answers About Joni Berman's Story and the**
  Story of OAPP (Primary Purpose)
  http://www.mediafire.com/?oy2vmbitzmh
- **AA Speakers**
  http://www.ppgaadallas.org/aa_speakers.htm

- **AA Speakers**
  Click on AA Cliff Bishop
  http://www.mediafire.com/sobrietyfirst jonib825
  http://www.dannyschwarzhoff.net/screens/speakers.swf
- AA Speakers
  Topics include: Pioneers - 12 Steps - 12 Traditions - 12 Concepts -
  Sponsorship
  Passing It On
  http://www.aaprimarypurpose.org/speakers.htm
- AA Speakers
  http://www.xa-speakers.org/
- Audio -- PPG Dallas Anniversary Talks
  http://www.mediafire.com/
  ?sharekey=a2194263c7a02e959bf8d6369220dcab11723ed53b13d9b
  a4d71ee60c1ce7296
- Audio -- PPG Dallas Traditions Talks
  http://www.mediafire.com/
  ?sharekey=a2194263c7a02e959bf8d6369220dcab09605c257b6abc
  d479b5ba51986ba

What is approved literature?
- **Big Book Concordance**
  Free online concordance of the BB
  http://www.royy.com/concord.html
- **Big Book Download download a searchable version (e-aa lite is free)**
  http://anonpress.org/choices/
- **Big Book Index Search the Big Book!**
  http://anonpress.org/bb/index.htm
- **Big Book Online Big Book you can read online**
  http://www.recovery.org/aa/bigbook/ww/
- **Big Book Search Search the first 164 pages of the Big Book**
  http://whytehouse.com/big_book_search/
- **Big Book Study Edition - A Big Book with blank pages for writing**
  http://anonpress.org/store/
- **Joe & Charlie Big Book Study**
  http://silkworth.net/freestuff.html
- **The Primary Purpose Group of Alcoholics Anonymous - Dallas, Texas**
  The Group OAPP is Modeled After: http://www.ppgaadallas.org/
- **Send an email to** oapp-subscribe@yahoogroups.com **or join at**
  http://health.groups.yahoo.com/group/oapp/links

Where can I buy the approved literature?
- http://bookstore.oa.org/quickform.php;
- http://www.oa.org
- http://www.aa.org
- http://www.amazon.com **and other bookstores**

The Coffee Shop

712-432-3900 Access PIN: 897578#
Daily - 7 A.M. EST
Recorded meeting:
712-432-3903 Access PIN: 897578#
Press 0# for most recent recording

Is there free downloadable literature?
- **Yes**

Where do I get free downloadable literature?
- **Big Book Download download a searchable version (e-aa lite is free)**
  http://anonpress.org/choices/

What is approved literature?
- **Alcoholics Anonymous, 4th Edition**
- **AA Approved Literature**
- **OA Approved Literature**
- **Big Book Concordance**
  Free online concordance of the BB
  http://www.royy.com/concord.html
- **Big Book Download download a searchable version (e-aa lite is free)**
  http://anonpress.org/choices/

Where can I buy the approved literature?
- http://bookstore.oa.org/quickform.php;
- http://www.oa.org
- http://www.aa.org
- http://www.amazon.com **and other bookstores**

The Parking Lot

Daily-712-432-3900
Access PIN: 6508933#
1 A.M. - 6:30 A.M. EST

What is approved literature?

- **People may read from any literature, including from their own writings. People may share stories, poems, their own writings, or any literature of their choice related to recovery. There is no restriction to AA-approved or OA-approved literature.**

Cups & Scales

http://groups.yahoo.com/group/cupsscalesgroup
cupsscalesgroup-subscribe@yahoogroups.com

What is approved literature?

- **'Cups & Scales' takes its name from the book *Cups & Scales, Weighing & Measuring Food & Emotions* by Anonymous Twelve Step Recovery Members. This book is after the famous AA-book *Stools & Bottles* that discusses character defects of the alcoholic. *Cups & Scales - Weighing & Measuring Food & Emotions - Information & Picture Book* is a serious picture Book with humor on character defects related to life and food trickery. It is recommended literature. *Cups & Scales Cookbook - Everything Weighed & Measured - Recipes - No Sugar, Wheat, Flour & Sample Plans of Eating* is recommended literature.**
- **'We are not a glum lot' it says in the AA Big Book. With our food trickery and curious twists of mind, we aim to become aware of how the body and mind are involved. When the food is "talking ", share to become aware of thoughts and attitudes. - fighting, defiance, rebellion, self-pity, and faulty glasses. The group takes no position on weighing and measuring food (http://groups. yahoo.com/group/cupsscalesgroup).**

Where can I buy the approved literature?

- http://www.amazon.com **and other bookstores**

Overeaters Anonymous Inc. (OA)

http://www.oa.org
PO Box 44020
Rio Rancho, New Mexico 87174-4020 USA
http://www.oa.org/contact.php
505-891-2664

- "Overeaters Anonymous is a fellowship of individuals who, through shared experience, strength, and hope are recovering from compulsive eating and compulsive eating behaviors. There are no dues or fees for members; members are self-supporting through their own contributions, neither soliciting nor accepting outside donations. OA is not affiliated with any public or private organization, political movement, ideology, or religious doctrine; it takes no position on outside issues. OA's primary purpose is to abstain from compulsive eating and to carry the message of recovery to those who still suffer. The group is open to everyone. The only requirement for membership is a desire to stop eating compulsively.

- Who belongs to OA? In Overeaters Anonymous, you'll find members who are extremely overweight, even morbidly obese; moderately overweight; average weight; underweight; still maintaining periodic control; or totally unable to control their compulsive eating. OA members experience many different patterns of food behaviors. These 'symptoms' are as varied as our membership. Among them are: • obsession with body weight, size and shape • eating binges or grazing • preoccupation with reducing diets • starving • laxative or diuretic abuse • excessive exercise • inducing vomiting after eating • chewing and spitting out food • use of diet pills, shots and other medical interventions to control weight • inability to stop eating certain foods after taking the first bite • fantasies about food • vulnerability to quick-weight-loss schemes • constant preoccupation with food • using food as a reward or comfort. Our symptoms may vary, but OA participants share a common bond: we are powerless over food and our lives are unmanageable. This common problem has led those in OA to seek and find a common solution in the Twelve Steps, the Twelve traditions and eight tools of Overeaters Anonymous. The only requirement for membership is 'a desire to stop compulsively overeating.'

- Overeaters Anonymous neither endorses nor supports any specific plan of eating. The OA pamphlet 'Dignity of Choice' explains different plans of eating and recommends that an individual work with their nutritionist or healthcare practitioner in choosing a plan of eating as part of a personal plan of recovery.

- The organization's definition of abstinence is 'refraining from compulsive eating.' Face-to-face meetings, phone meetings, and online meetings are open to everyone.

- Everyone may request a Phone Buddy, Action Partner or Sponsor. The "Nine Tools" in Overeaters Anonymous are: plan of eating, sponsorship, telephone, meetings, writing, literature, anonymity, service, and plan of action" (Overeaters Anonymous Inc, 2010, http://www.oa.org).

Organizations

CEA-HOW (Compulsive Overeaters Anonymous-HOW)

http://www.ceahow.org/
5500 E. Atherton St., Suite 227-B
Long Beach, CA 90815-4017
562-342-9344
CEA-HOW General Service Office: gso@ceahow

- "Compulsive Eaters Anonymous-HOW is a fellowship of individuals who, through shared experience, strength, and hope are recovering from compulsive eating and food addiction. We welcome everyone who wants to stop eating compulsively. There are no dues or fees for members; we are self-supporting through our own contributions, neither soliciting nor accepting outside donations. CEA-HOW is not affiliated with any public or private organization, political movement, ideology, or religious doctrine; we take no position on outside issues. Our primary purpose is to abstain from compulsive eating and to carry the message of recovery to those who still suffer. The Compulsive Eaters Anonymous-HOW Concept has been formed to offer the compulsive eater who accepts the Twelve Steps and Twelve Traditions as a program of recovery a disciplined and structured approach.

  The CEA-HOW Groups have been formed in the belief that our disease is absolute and therefore only absolute acceptance of the CEA-HOW Concept will offer any sustained abstinence to those of us whose compulsion has reached a critical level. Therefore, the CEA-HOW plan of eating, steps, traditions and tools of recovery are not suggested. Rather, we accept them as requirements for our recovery (http://www.ceahow.org). Note: CEA-HOW is not affiliated with Overeaters Anonymous or the OA-HOW meetings, where refraining from sugar and flour or following a specific plan of eating is a suggestion and not a requirement" (CEA-HOW Website, http://www.ceahow.org, May 2010).

  There is a required plan of eating. It includes fruit, dairy, protein and vegetables. The CEA-HOW plan of eating is available from "Achieving Balance Cookbook" at the website:
  http://www.ceahow.org/?q=node/11

Food Addicts Anonymous, Inc.

http://www.foodaddictsanonymous.org/meetings-events
561-967-3871

- "Food Addicts Anonymous Inc., founded in 1987, is a group of individuals helping one another, based on a belief that food addiction is a bio-chemical disease. By following a food plan devoid of all addictive substances, we can recover. These substances include sugar, flour, and wheat in all their forms. They also include fats and any other high-carbohydrate, refined, processed foods that cause us problems individually. You need to know that withdrawal is a necessary part of recovery. We can get better if we continue to follow our food plan, work the tools of the program, and ask for help.

"Food Addicts Anonymous is a fellowship of men and women who are willing to recover from the disease of food addiction. Sharing our experience, strength, and hope with others allows us to recover from this disease, one day at a time. Our primary purpose is to stay abstinent and to help other food addicts achieve abstinence. We invite you to join us on the road to recovery and suggest you attend six meetings before you decide you don't need our help. Food Addicts Anonymous is self-supporting through our own contributions. We are not affiliated with any diet or weight loss programs, treatment facilities, or religious organizations. We neither endorse nor oppose any causes. Our primary purpose is to stay abstinent and to help other food addicts achieve abstinence. Food Addicts Anonymous was founded in December of 1987, by Judith C. in West Palm Beach, Florida (http://www.foodaddictsanonymous.org website, May 2010)."

There is an FAA plan of eating. It includes fruit, dairy, protein, vegetables, and starches and grains. People follow a food plan devoid of all addictive substances, including sugar, flour and wheat in all their forms. These substances also include fats and any other high-carbohydrate, refined, processed foods that cause problems individually. The FAA plan of eating is found on the website:
http://www.foodaddictsanonymous.org/faa-food-plan.

Organizations

The Recovery Group

http://www.therecoverygroup.org/

- "The Recovery Group is a 12 Step community for men and women who have the desire to quit eating compulsively. Our extensive program includes email discussion lists, both general and special focus, online OA meetings, Big Book and Step Studies, registered OA phone meetings, and a Sponsor Program, special writings program and many other services. You are invited to join us on our recovery journey.

  There are over 60 discussion groups, referred to as "loops" here. People love receiving email communications from other compulsive eaters. This resource was founded in 1995. It allows people to share around specific issues. When you join by going to the website: http://www.therecoverygroup.org, you will start to receive posts from other people who belong to the loop; you will be able to post your message, writing, or thoughts.

- Vital online discussion groups or "loops" exist for: AGE: Kids, Teens, Silver (over 50); CROSS-ADDICTION: AA, Anger, Drug Abuse, Love and Sex, Spending; FAITH: Christian, Jewish, Latterday Saints, Pagan; FAMILY & FRIENDS: Abuse, CoKids, Divorce, FFOA Grief, Isolation, OA Anon, Parenting, Rainbow To Abstinence, Relationships, FOOD BASED: Abstinence, The Abstinent Kitchen, HEALTH: Anorexia/Bulimia, Cancer, Depression, Diabetes, Disabilities, Emotions, Homebound, Isolation, Pain, PMS, Pregnancy & Motherhood, Weight Loss Surgery; INTERNATIONAL: Deutchland OA, Espana OA, France OA, Israel, Italia OA; PROGRAM RELATED: 90 In 90, Abstinence, Grey Sheet, HOW, Journey to Recovery, Meditations & Recovery, OAFriends, OA Newcomers, OARecovery, OAsis, Relapse, Sponsor/Sponsee Talk, Strong Recovery, The Big Book, WTS; SPECIAL INTEREST: Creative, Exercise, The Yellow Brick Road; WEIGHT RELATED: 200 Plus, Hot J, Weight Loss Surgery.

- The Recovery Group OA Online Meetings are held every three hours daily, at 12 noon, 3, 6, 9, 12 midnight, and 3 a.m. 6, a.m. and 9 a.m. EST" (The Recovery Group Statement, June 2010, http://www.therecoverygroup.org.)

- There is no required plan of eating. This resource abides by the OA "The Dignity of Choice" pamphlet with openness and non-endorsement of any particular plan of eating. People can choose a plan of eating if they want to. They can talk about and identify their food, eating, and life issues.

- There are available Sponsors and Email Angels.
  Go to: http://www.therecoverygroup.org/sponsors.html or send an email to: Sponsors@TheRecoveryGroup.org.

Greysheeters Anonymous (GSA)

http://www.greysheet.org/cms/
GSA World Services or GSAWS, Inc.
Cherokee Station
PO Box 20098
New York, NY 10021-0061
uscontacts@greysheet.org
phonelist@greysheet.org

- Greysheeters Anonymous Inc., founded in 1998, is made up of individuals who strongly support the Greysheet Food Plan, weighing and measuring food, and communicating with a sponsor, as a method to recover from compulsive eating.

- "GreySheeters Anonymous is a fellowship of men and women who share their experience, strength, and hope with each other that they may solve their common problem and help others to recover from compulsive overeating. The group is open to everyone. The only requirement for membership is the desire to stop eating compulsively. There are no dues or fees for GSA membership; we are self-supporting through our own contributions. GSA is not allied with any sect, denomination, politics, organization, or institution; does not wish to engage in any controversy; neither endorses nor opposes any causes. Our primary purpose is to stay abstinent and help other compulsive overeaters to achieve abstinence. GreySheeters Anonymous has been founded and designed to discuss the fundamentals or basics of attaining and maintaining GreySheet abstinence. For that purpose we explore together the program of Alcoholics Anonymous in arresting compulsive eating. We strongly support GreySheet. We require that our meeting leaders be abstinent for at least three months on the GreySheet.

  We support a vigorous and positive attitude toward GreySheet abstinence which we define as three weighed and measured meals a day from the GreySheet, with nothing in between but black coffee, tea, or diet soda. A 'Greysheet Food Plan' may be obtained by first getting a Greysheet Sponsor. A qualified GreySheet sponsor is someone who has at least 90 days of back-to- back, uninterrupted GS abstinence. (Greysheeters Anonymous Website, http://www.greysheet.org, May 2010).

Organizations

A list of available sponsors is available from: http://www.greysheet.org/cms/sponsors.html. A sponsor explains how to weigh and measure without exception from the GreySheet Food Plan and provides a copy of the GreySheet Food Plan. GreySheet abstinence is defined by Greysheet Anonymous as: • Weighing and measuring three meals a day from the GreySheet as explained by a qualified GreySheet sponsor, • Committing those meals to a qualified GreySheet sponsor before eating them, • Doing this without exception, i.e., there is no situation where we do not weigh and measure, • Eating or drinking nothing in between those three meals except black coffee, black tea, no-calorie soft drinks, or water (Greysheet Anonymous, http://www.greysheet.org)."

- There is a required plan of eating. The Greysheet plan of eating comes with a Sponsor.   The Greysheet food plan was originally offered for suggestion by Overeater's Anonymous Inc. in the 1960's, a very low carb, high protein food plan, no breads, flour products, only products that list sugar at least fifth on the label, and quantities suggested in weighed and measured amounts.

Food Addiction: The Body Knows

http://www.kaysheppard.com/
kshepp825@aol.com
321-727-8040
thebodyknows-subscribe@yahoogroups.com

- **"The Body Knows"** (thebodyknows-subscribe@yahoogroups.com) **is an online discussion group, with phone meetings, face- to-face meetings in Florida, and online meetings via online chat. It is a group of people who use the plan of eating suggested in the book** *Food Addiction: The Body Knows*, **1989 by Kay Sheppard. Started in 2000, the group is open to everyone; there are no requirements to join the group. People discuss how to use a "Recovery Food Plan" suggested by Kay Sheppard with the principles of 12 Step Recovery; how to recognize the dangers in so-called "health" foods; how to overcome emotional barriers to recovery; how to find recovery buddies; how to recognize the warning signs of relapse; and how to incorporate the Twelve Steps into your life to stay motivated and achieve success.**

  There is a suggested plan of eating. It includes fruit, dairy, protein, vegetables, and starches and grains. People follow a food plan devoid of all addictive substances, including sugar, flour and wheat in all their forms. These substances also include fats and any other high-carbohydrate, refined, processed foods that cause problems individually. is similar to the plan of eating recommended in Food Addicts Anonymous. It includes an additional serving of starch and grain at lunch. The plan of eating recommends no caffein, no sweeteners and weighed and measured servings. The plan of eating is found on the website: http://www.kaysheppard.com.

Organizations

Anorexics & Bulimics Anonymous

http://www.anorexicsandbulimicsanonymousaba.com/
Main P.O. Box 125 | Edmonton, AB T5J 2G9
780-443-6077

- "Anorexics and Bulimics Anonymous (ABA), founded in 2002, is a Fellowship of individuals whose primary purpose is to find and maintain 'sobriety' in our eating practices, and to help others gain sobriety.

  The only requirement for membership is a desire to stop unhealthy eating practices. There are no dues or fees for ABA membership; we are self-supporting through our own contributions. ABA is not affiliated with any other organization or institution, nor are we allied with any religion. ABA is a non-professional organization and is not therapy, nor is it intended to replace professional medical treatment. Anorexia and bulimia are serious and potentially fatal conditions whose physical manifestations must be corrected before there can be any hope for mental and spiritual recovery. We encourage all sufferers to also consult with qualified and knowledgeable health care professionals.

  ABA uses the Twelve-Step Program adapted from Alcoholics Anonymous to address the mental, emotional, and spiritual components of the disorders of anorexia and bulimia. By following the Twelve Steps we have come to a deep level of freedom from our deadly obsessions with body weight and shape and with food, obsessions that once dominated our minds and dictated the course of our lives. We learn in ABA that our eating disorders are a form of addiction, that the key to recovery is to find 'sobriety' in our eating and exercise and we cannot do that alone.

  In ABA we find the guidance and compassionate support of other anorexics and bulimics who have gone before us in recovery, and we receive the courage to surrender our unhealthy behavior patterns. Each of us comes to connect with a Higher Power of our own understanding, who heals our minds as we stay sober physically.

  Many people who identify compulsive overeating as the primary component of their eating disorder have been able to relate to our program and have found recovery through it. They are welcome to participate in our Fellowship" (http://anorexicsandbulemicsaba.com, May 2010).

12 Steps for Compulsive Overeaters (OA12StepsforCOES)
Online 12 Step Group for Compulsive Overeaters

OA Inc. Registered Intergroup
http://www.oa12step4coes.org
sunlight@oa12step4coes.org

- OA 12 Step for COES is an online circle that provides email discussion loops and online meetings. Founded in 2005 as an OA Inc. Intergroup, OA 12Step4COES hosts online chat meetings and email discussion groups, where Phone Buddies, Action Partners & Sponsors are available.

- There are online meetings for Moms, Males, Seniors and Teens. People love using the Chat Room to attend online meetings.

- There are special focus email discussion groups for Recovery 4 Relapse; Sponsors 4 Today; Healing Abuse & Compulsive Overeating; Chronic Illness or Injury and Compulsive Overeating; Emotional Health Issues and Compulsive Overeating; 12 Step 4 Christian Compulsive Overeaters; Rainbow 12 Step 4 Compulsive Overeaters; and 12 Step 4 Codependent Compulsive Overeaters. People love belonging to email discussion groups where they may post and talk with other participants about special issues.

"Overeaters Anonymous is a Fellowship of individuals who, through shared experience, strength and hope, are recovering from compulsive overeating. We welcome everyone who wants to stop eating compulsively. There are no dues or fees for members; we are self-supporting through our own contributions, neither soliciting nor accepting outside donations. OA is not affiliated with any public or private organization, political movement, ideology or religious doctrine; we take no position on outside issues. Our primary purpose is to abstain from compulsive overeating and to carry this message of recovery to those who still suffer" (http://www.oa12step4coes.org/oa.html, May 2010).

Recovery from Food Addiction (RFA)

http://health.groups.yahoo.com/group/recoveryfromfoodaddiction/
recoveryfromfoodaddiction-subscribe@yahoogroups.com
P.O. Box 35543
713-673-2848

- **Recovery from Food Addiction hosts a phone meeting, face-to-face meetings and an online email discussion group** (recoveryfromfoodaddiction-subscribe@yahoogroups.

- **"Recovery from Food Addiction is a Twelve Step Anonymous Program that addresses the disease of food addiction. Our primary purpose is to stay abstinent from the addictive substances of sugar, flour, and wheat and to help others to do the same. Abstinence from sugar, flour, and wheat is the foundation of our program of recovery...**

  We believe we eat because of a physical craving; that we have an addiction to certain foods. The addictive substances set up an insatiable craving within our bodies. The only relief from the craving is entire abstinence from these foods. We believe that we do not eat because of our problems; however, if we do not keep in a fit spiritual condition by working the 12 steps of this program, we will go back to the food .

  There is a suggested plan of eating. *Food Addiction: The Body Knows* **by Kay Sheppard is approved literature. The food plan in the book is recommended. It includes fruit, dairy, protein, vegetables, and starches and grains. People follow a food plan devoid of all addictive substances, including sugar, flour and wheat in all their forms. These substances also include fats and any other high-carbohydrate, refined, processed foods that cause problems individually. is similar to the plan of eating recommended in Food Addicts Anonymous. It includes an additional serving of starch/grain at lunch. The plan of eating recommends no caffein, no sweeteners and weighed and measured servings. The plan of eating is found on the website:** http://www.kaysheppard.com. **If you currently have a plan that is free of the addictive substances of sugar, flour, and wheat, and it is working, you may continue to use it. We recommend that you always check with your doctor before starting any food plan. (**http://health.groups.yahoo.com/group/recoveryfromfoodaddiction/)".

Organizations

OA Primary Purpose

http://www.oapp.info/oaprimarypurposegroups
http://health.groups.yahoo.com/group/oapp/links
oapp-subscribe@yahoogroups.com
To Request an Invitation to Join: Send an email to: jonip@oapp.info
712-432-3900 PIN 643578#

- "OA Primary purpose is an OA group/community that is modeled after the AA primary purpose. The leader is Joni P. Send an email to Joni P. at joni@oapp.info to request to join. OA Primary Purpose is an open membership study group that uses the online technology of SKYPE to host conference calls for daily phone meetings. Each group has but one primary purpose — to carry its message to the compulsive eater who still suffers. We are a fellowship of people who have recovered from the illness of compulsive eating by following the program of action laid out in the book Alcoholics Anonymous.

- Our purpose is simple, clear, and outlined above. We are compulsive eaters and our experience is that following the directions precisely out of the Big Book saved our lives; taking the Twelve Steps swiftly and thoroughly with the guidance of a sponsor and helping other compulsive eaters in turn. We use the AA Big Book as our text, studying it in meetings and with our sponsors, because following the simple program of action in the Big Book is how we recovered. We bring our experience and knowledge of recovery to our meetings, and bring our fears, resentments and worries to our sponsors. If compulsive eating is a problem for you we welcome you. If you have sat in therapy groups and discussion meetings, not taking the steps and wondering why you're not getting better, we welcome you.

- This is an open membership group, which uses 'The Primary Purpose Group Big Book Study Guide', developed by The Primary Purpose Group of Alcoholics Anonymous, Dallas, TX to do a line by line study of our basic text. As in any OA group, the only requirement for membership in OAPP is the desire to stop eating compulsively.

- Each morning the moderator will post questions which can be answered by a line in the text. Later that day, the moderator will post the answers. We invite you to share your experience and knowledge with the portion of the text being studied. You will need a sponsor to guide you through the program of recovery as outlined in the Big Book. We recommend that you find one from the Recovered Member List by clicking on 'Database'. 'When the spiritual malady is overcome, we straighten out mentally and physically.'(BB p. 64)", (OAPP Statement, June 2010, http://health.groups.yahoo.com/group/oapp/links).

The Coffee Shop

> 712-432-3900 Access PIN: 897578#
> Daily - 7 A.M. EST
> Recorded meeting:
> 712-432-3903 Access PIN: 897578#
> Press 0# for most recent recording
> Code for previous recording

- Started in 2007, The Coffee Shop is an OA-type meeting moderated by Andre P. It lasts for one hour. People are invited to share on the reading and topic. The meetings are recorded. People are invited to listen to the recording of the meeting by calling 712-432-3903 PIN 897578# and pressing 0#. The access PIN for the previous day's recorded meeting is given each day at 7 a.m. 7 a.m. phone meeting.

Organizations

The Parking Lot

    712-432-3900
    Access PIN: 6508933#
    Daily - 1 A.M. - 6:30 A.M. EST

- Started in 2010, The Parking Lot is an all-night open phone discussion. It goes from 1 a.m. to 6:30 a.m. or later EST. You can adjust the times for your time zone. The discussion is not an official meeting of any organization. It follows an open discussion format. There is a moderator. It is moderated by Irene and others.

- People do readings, poetry, music, and open sharing. The discussion is for night-eaters, night workers, people who eat in the middle of the night, or people who want recovery. Other 12 step programs such as Debtors Anonymous, Clutters Anonymous, or others may be discussed. The emphasis is on recovery.

- People talk on topics such as daily struggles, insights, lessons, and anything related to recovery. The purpose is to save lives. People share phone numbers and emails to receive outreach calls.

Cups & Scales

http://groups.yahoo.com/group/cupsscalesgroup
cupsscalesgroup-subscribe@yahoogroups.com

- "Cups & Scales is an online discussion group (cupsscalesgroup-subscribe@yahoogroups.com), **started in 2010, to discuss attitudes around life and food trickery. Distorted eating often begins with distorted thinking.**

- 'Cups & Scales' takes its name from the book *Cups & Scales, Weighing & Measuring Food & Emotions* by Anonymous Twelve Step Recovery Members. This book is after the famous AA-book *Stools & Bottles* that discusses character defects of the alcoholic. *Cups & Scales - Weighing & Measuring Food & Emotions - Information & Picture Book* is a serious picture Book with humor on character defects related to life and food trickery. It is **recommended literature.** *Cups & Scales Cookbook - Everything Weighed & Measured - Recipes - No Sugar, Wheat, Flour & Sample Plans of Eating* is recommended literature.

  'We are not a glum lot' it says in the AA Big Book. With our food trickery and curious twists of mind, we aim to become aware of how the body and mind are involved. When the food is "talking ", we share to become aware of thoughts and attitudes. - fighting, defiance, rebellion, self-pity, and faulty glasses. The group takes no position on weighing and measuring. This group is open to all. People are invited to talk about food trickery, character defects, problems, or tools and thinking (http://groups.yahoo.com/group/cupsscalesgroup)."